MEDIEVALISM

GEORGE TYRRELL (1861-1909) was born in Dublin of Anglican parents. Under the influence of Robert Dolling, an Anglo-Catholic social reformer, Tyrrell was drawn as an adolescent to Roman Catholicism. At Dolling's invitation he left Dublin for London in 1879. The following year he was received into the Roman Catholic Church at the Jesuit Farm Street church in London and shortly afterwards entered the Jesuits. He studied philosophy at Stonyhurst in Lancashire and theology at St Beuno's in Wales. He was ordained in 1891. After a short period in a Lancashire parish, he was sent to teach philosophy at Stonyhurst, where his sponsoring of pure Thomism against Suarezianism caused tension among his colleagues. As a result he was removed from Stonyhurst and sent to Farm Street as a writer. In 1897 he met Baron Friedrich von Hügel who, by introducing him to German and French scholarship, had a profound effect on his intellectual development. Almost from the start of his writing career, Tyrrell had difficulties with the censors and was reduced to writing anonymously or under pseudonym. In 1906 he was expelled from the Jesuits on the instructions of Pope Pius X. After the publication of the encyclical *Pascendi*, condemning "modernism," Tyrrell wrote two defiant articles and was consequently excomminicated. He died at Storrington in Susse ' in July 1909, was refused a Catholic burial, and is buried in the Anglican cemetery there.

MEDIEVALISM

A REPLY TO CARDINAL MERCIER

BY

GEORGE TYRRELL

With a Foreword by
GABRIEL DALY, O.S.A.

As level clouds that blush to fiery red
When the day dies, or rises from the dead,
Saw I the face of Heaven with shame o'er spread.
DANTE, *Paradiso* xxvii. 25

Christian Classics
A DIVISION OF THOMAS MORE PUBLISHING

Allen, Texas • Chicago, Illinois

This edition published 1994
BURNS & OATES
Wellwood, North Farm Road,
Tunbridge Wells, Kent TN2 3DR

American edition 1994
published by
CHRISTIAN CLASSICS
A division of Thomas More Publishing,
200 East Bethany Drive, Allen, Texas 75002-3804

*First published by Longmans, Green, and Co., London,
New York, Bombay and Calcutta, 1908. This edition
reprinted from the Third Impression, with additions, 1909.*

Foreword © Copyright Burns & Oates Limited 1994

ISBN 0 87061 207 7

Composition by Search Press Limited
Printed and bound in Great Britain by
Biddles Ltd, Guildford and King's Lynn

CONTENTS

FOREWORD by GABRIEL DALY, O.S.A.   *Page* 7

THE LENTEN PASTORAL   21

A REPLY TO CARDINAL MERCIER   35

    I. THE IMMUNITY OF BELGIUM   39

    II. THE SUPPOSED ESSENCE OF MODERNISM   45

    III. THE SUPPOSED ESSENCE OF CATHOLICISM   49

    IV. THE SUPPOSED CONSTITUTION OF THE CHURCH   58

    V. GROWTH OF THIS CONCEPTION   70

    VI. THE VATICAN DEFINITION   79

    VII. "THE APOSTATE DÖLLINGER"   87

    VIII. THE SUPPOSED ESSENCE OF PROTESTANTISM   93

    IX. A SUPPOSED LEADER OF MODERNISM   100

    X. HIS INDIFFERENCE TO HISTORY AND DOGMA   102

    XI. HIS KANTIAN PREPOSSESSIONS   104

    XII. HIS DARWINIAN PREPOSSESSIONS   107

    XIII. HIS INDIVIDUALIST PREPOSSESSIONS   110

    XIV. MODERNISM AND SCIENTIFIC FREEDOM   113

    XV. MODERNISM AND POPULAR GOVERNMENT   121

    XVI. ONE ASPECT OF MODERNISM   132

CONTENTS

XVII. OTHER ASPECTS OF MODERNISM   145

XVIII. POSSIBLE TRANSFORMATIONS
          OF MODERNISM   148

 XIX. THE DEATH-AGONY OF
          MEDIEVALISM   155

  XX. THE MORAL ROOT OF THE
          CONFLICT   162

 XXI. CONCLUSION   165

NOTE   170

FOREWORD
BY GABRIEL DALY, O.S.A.

In Lent of 1908 Desiré Mercier, Cardinal Archbishop of
Malines and Primate of Belgium, addressed a Pastoral
Letter to his people on the subject of modernism. The
pastoral was published less than a year after the papal
condemnation of what was designated a new heresy to
which Rome had given the name "modernism." The papal
encyclical, *Pascendi Dominici Gregis*, had prescribed a large-
scale counter-offensive against what it claimed was an
extremely serious campaign to undermine the faith of the
Church from the inside. The Roman authorities made it
very plain that they expected dedicated co-operation from
the world's bishops and that any lack of inquisitorial
enthusiasm would be unfavourably noted. Cardinal
Mercier's lenten pastoral was a clear response to the call to
arms.

The pastoral informed the faithful of Malines that Belgium was blessedly free from the new errors. The faithful
may have wondered why in that case their learned archbishop had thought it necessary to speak to them about
those errors. Their wonder can hardly have lessened
when, almost half-way through the letter, they were told
that "the most penetrating observer of the present Modernist movement—the one most alive to its tendencies,
who has best divined its spirit, and is perhaps more
deeply imbued with it than any other, is the English priest
Tyrrell."

Tyrrell was the only modernist named in the pastoral.
This is intriguing in view of the fact that the errors
condemned by Rome had been drawn in the main from
Alfred Loisy's writings. While it is true that some of
Tyrrell's work had been translated into French, it is hardly

7

likely that Mercier thought him more dangerous to the people of Belgium than Loisy, Houtin or Hébert. The solution to this puzzle is to be found in the devious world of ecclesiastical politics. Some historical background is necessary for an understanding of what happened.

In 1906 Father George Tyrrell was expelled from the Society of Jesus in spite of the efforts made on his behalf by his English superiors. He had been having difficulties with the censors, local and Roman, over his writings. As a result, he had resorted to either anonymous or pseudonymous publication. His authorship of these publications was known to some and guessed by others. Becoming increasingly convinced of the untenability of his position as a Jesuit, he began to explore the possibility of leaving the Society in a manner that would satisfy the requirements of canon law and his own sense of honour. This meant embroilment in the complicated, not to say byzantine, procedures of a Roman bureaucracy within which different departments were keeping a wary eye on each other in full awareness that their ultimate master, Pope Pius X, had embarked with grim determination on a crusade to purge the Church of what he saw as the insidious dangers of theological liberalism.

Matters came to a head with the publication in the Milan *Corriere della Sera* of some excerpts from Tyrrell's privately circulated *A Letter to a University Professor*.[1] The Archbishop of Milan wrote to the Jesuit General, Luis Martín, who in turn wrote to Tyrrell asking him if he was the author. Tyrrell conceded that he was the author but disclaimed responsibility for the translation and publication. Martín sought, but failed to obtain, a retraction from Tyrrell. In February 1906, under instruction from the Pope himself,[2] Father Martín dismissed him from the Society.

A major problem for Tyrrell was how and where to find an *episcopus benevolus*, that is, a bishop willing to take him into his diocese. Both Archbishop Bourne of Westminster and Archbishop Walsh of Dublin told him that they had a policy of not incardinating ex-regulars in their dioceses. The Archbishop of San Francisco was willing to take him, but Tyrrell, while grateful, felt that that was too far away.[3]

Tyrrell had more friends and well-wishers than he realized. One of these well-wishers was Dom Columba Marmion, abbot of Maredsous in Belgium. Marmion approached Archbishop Mercier of Malines who expressed interest and commissioned Mother Mary Stanislaus, Prioress of the English Convent in Bruges, who knew Tyrrell through his retreat-giving, to ask him if he would be willing to come to Belgium, where he would find an *episcopus benevolus*. There were conditions, however. Tyrrell must not preach, hear confessions, or publish anything without the bishop's authorization. Tyrrell replied, "I must be received on the ordinary footing or not at all."[4] Having heard of this from Mother Mary Stanislaus, Mercier asked her to enquire of Tyrrell whether he wished Mercier to intercede for him with Rome. Tyrrell wrote back, "Don't ask him to do anything; he will injure himself and not help me." Unknown to Tyrrell, however, Mercier decided to write to Cardinal Merry del Val, Secretary of State at the Vatican, who sent his letter on to Cardinal Ferrata, Prefect of the Congregation of Bishops and Religious. Ferrata authorized Mercier to receive Tyrrell into his archdiocese on condition that Tyrrell would "pledge himself formally not to publish anything on religious matters nor to engage in epistolary correspondence without the previous approval of a competent person designated "by the archbishop."[5] Mercier thought these conditions reasonable. Tyrrell, needless to say, did not. He was, however, grateful for the archbishop's solicitude. Mercier then wrote for the first time directly to Tyrrell, addressing him as *"mon cher confrère dans le sacerdoce,"* and asking him to reconsider his rejection of the conditions. Tyrrell wrote back through Mother Mary Stanislaus remarking how touched he was but reiterating his refusal of the conditions, especially the censoring of his "epistolary correspondence,"

9

which, he claimed, was mainly with "Catholic priests and prelates of unsuspected but tottering orthodoxy; with seminarians and their professors; with religious and their bewildered superiors, with teachers, writers etc.," in short, with people who relied on his discretion and care for confidentiality.[6] There matters rested, with Tyrrell still in need of a bishop but grateful to Mercier for his interest. The modernist crisis was now moving to its climax and several events were to affect Tyrrell directly.

On 17 April 1907 Pius X addressed five new cardinals, one of whom was the archbishop of Malines, exhorting them to take energetic action against the novel and dangerous ideas abroad in the Church. On 3 July the Holy office published the decree *Lamentabili*, which listed the errors that were believed to be threatening the Church. This was the new "syllabus," reminiscent of Pius IX's notorious "Syllabus of Errors" of 1864 which had declared war on modernity of every kind. On 8 September Pius X issued his encyclical, *Pascendi Dominici Gregis*, which presented a systematic account of the new errors and prescribed draconian measures to deal with those deemed to hold them.

The encyclical caused an immediate crisis throughout the Catholic Church. It inaugurated a period of ecclesiastical McCarthyism when "modernists" were hunted down with a zeal that was as pathological as the paranoia that fed it. Bemused bishops throughout the Church were exhorted to ferret out offenders. Seminary professors were disturbed to find themselves potentially suspect of a heresy of which many of them had no intelligence and about which their teaching manuals had, as yet, nothing to say. Vigilance committees met in solemn conclave to determine who was guilty, or at least suspect, of this newest and most nebulous of heresies. Career-orientated priests denounced their colleagues. A climate of fear prevailed throughout the Church. There were many anxious huddles and much running for cover. Many Catholic scholars agonized over whether they or their friends had been hit by the papal onslaught. Friendships, including that between Tyrrell and von Hügel, were put under severe strain. The Baron, who knew his friend too well to expect reticence and ecclesiastical trimming from him, was shortly to have his worst fears realized.

Tyrrell accepted requests from the *Giornale d'Italia* and *The Times* to express his views on the new encyclical. Both articles were fiercely critical, and Tyrrell himself was well aware that they amounted to an act of ecclesiastical suicide, thus spectacularly bearing out what he had once written to Robert Dell: "I am a mere gander in diplomacy. ... My own impulse is always to cut off my head and fling it at my enemy's head—which I admit is poor play, and just what my enemy wants."[7] He was then living mainly in Storrington in Sussex, and so it fell to the bishop of Southwark, Peter Amigo, to react to the *Times* articles and to become the agent of Roman retribution. Amigo wrote to Tyrrell on 22 October 1907, informing him that the Holy See had given instructions that he was to be deprived of the sacraments by reason of the *Times* articles and that his case had been reserved to Rome.

The last two years of his life were spent under what amounted to excommunication. (Unlike Loisy, however, he was not publicly named or declared *vitandus*, i.e., someone to be shunned by all his fellow Catholics). He made no move to leave the Church—a decision that many people then and since have wondered about. He considered returning to the Church of his baptism, but, in the event, decided against it. He told his Anglican friends that returning to the Church of his childhood would indeed bring a momentary peace, but it would mean abandoning what he believed had become his special vocation. It would be a betrayal of those Roman Catholics who looked to him for help and inspiration in their present anguish.

On 12 November 1907 Cardinal Mercier sent to Rome a submission to the anti-modernist documents by the University of Louvain, by diocesan seminaries, and by congregations of teaching religious. In December he made an official visit to the University and spoke against modernism.[8] The following year he wrote his Lenten Pastoral on modernism singling out *"le prêtre anglais Tyrrell"* for exclusive mention and condemnation.

When Tyrrell learned about the Pastoral Letter he was outraged by the utterly gratuitous mention of his name in it. On 25 April 1908 he wrote to Mercier:

> Your Eminence,
>
> It is by a mere chance that I have just learnt the purpose of your Lenten Pastoral.
>
> I shall reply to it in the course of a few weeks in the form of a small volume. As I wish to be perfectly fair to Your Eminence, I trust you will allow me to print your Pastoral in the Appendix. If however you decline, or do not reply, I shall put a note to that effect, with a copy of this letter.
>
> Your Eminence's
> obedient servant
> G. Tyrrell[9]

Mercier wrote back agreeing to Tyrrell's printing of the pastoral on condition that he gave the full text "at least of that portion that concerns you."

The "small volume" was written in something like six weeks. It was powered by all the emotions that had been building up in Tyrrell and that were now being brought to white heat by a sense of betrayal on the part of someone whom he had respected and believed to be well disposed toward him. He knew that by singling him out for special mention Mercier was seeking to make amends to Rome for his earlier friendliness toward someone who was now execrated in Roman curial circles as one of the foremost modernist leaders. Mercier's act represented all that Tyrrell detested in ecclesiastical life, "the need and desire of saying the orthodox thing that leads to a certain inward insincerity or lack of openmindedness."[10] He placed an outstandingly high value on the virtue of courage and he felt that the prevailing ideas on obedience and authority were promoting cowardice, insincerity and hypocrisy in the Church. He knew that ecclesiastics like Mercier were saying one thing in private and another in public,[11] but he allowed nothing of this to appear in *Medievalism*, a book which observes all the decencies of debate, even if it offended against the ecclesiastical conventions then obtaining between priest and prelate.

Medievalism was an immediate *succès de scandale*. Although Tyrrell did not wish it to be the book by which he would be remembered, it is nevertheless a faithful reflection of his most typical attitudes and convictions. In it he produces a masterly blend of rhetoric, history, and theology. Its principal themes were second nature to him by the time he came to write it; and they were still developing. At its heart lies the distinction that he had drawn almost ten years earlier between revelation and theology.[12] In his *Times* comments on *Pascendi* he had remarked that "When the encyclical tries to show the modernist that he is no Catholic, it mostly succeeds only in showing him that he is no scholastic—which he knew."

The protest against revelation as statement is coupled with an equally strong protest against what Blondel had called "extrinsicism", the absence of an immanent, experiential, dimension in the Neo-scholastic idea of revelation, faith and church life. Neo-scholastic apologetics was based not on inner experience but on the extrinsic "proofs" provided by miracles and fulfilled prophecies. These were taken as external authentications of the truths taught by revelation and enshrined in church dogma. The message was seen as being addressed to faith from the outside. Any appeal to an inner dimension as a necessary prerequisite for revelation to occur was dismissed as Protestant subjectivism and individualism which, as Mercier says in his

Pastoral Letter, are "substituted for the Catholic conception of a teaching authority officially established by Jesus Christ, and commissioned to tell us what, under pain of eternal damnation, we are compelled to believe." The integralist case could hardly have been put more crudely. Tyrrell's refutation of it is devastating.

Tyrrell, moreover, linked this lack of an interior and truly social and consultative conception of church with the centralized authoritarianism that he attacks in *Medievalism*. He saw democratic attitudes and procedures as instruments of the Holy Spirit present in the whole Church and not merely in its leaders. His opposition to papal hegemony was not merely ecclesiological; it arose out of his conviction that the sort of centralization that gave the pope virtually absolute power, while identifying the papacy with one narrow theological party and denying a hearing to all others, obstructed the channels through which the Holy Spirit communicated with the Church. Long before collegiality had become an important issue in the twentieth century Catholic Church Tyrrell was protesting, as he does here, against the notion that bishops are papal delegates, priests episcopal delegates, and laity passive recipients of clerical instruction. In *Medievalism* he argues that the tendency to confuse theology and faith, long present in the Church, was deliberately intensified after the First Vatican Council in an effort to promote uniformity through verbal orthodoxy.

Mercier in his Lenten Pastoral coupled Tyrrell's name with that of Ignaz von Döllinger, the distinguished Bavarian church historian who opposed the definition of papal infallibility made at the First Vatican Council. Tyrrell expresses his admiration for Döllinger but does not follow him in his rejection of the validity of the council on the grounds that it was neither free, representative nor unanimous. Tyrrell rightly appreciates that such an objection would invalidate most, if not all, Church councils. Instead he proposes an embryonic theory of conciliar hermeneutics. If biblical criticism has made it impossible to read scripture in a pre-critical manner, he remarks, then, *a fortiori*, conciliar statements call for historico-critical interpretation. He therefore accepts Strossmayer's view that the hard-line ultramontanes had failed to commit the Church to their own private theological interpretation of papal power. Nevertheless the ultramontane interpretation had, since 1870, prevailed as the only allowable orthodoxy. It is this post-Vatican I theology that Tyrrell describes throughout *Medievalism* as "the new theology" When it is identified with Christian revelation, he calls the result "theologism."[13]

Although the term "modernism" was first used by its Roman opponents, Tyrrell had no problem accepting and working with it. In general terms he describes it as the conviction that Catholic faith is compatible with modern culture. In chapter XVI of *Medievalism* he writes: "Medievalism is an absolute, Modernism a relative term. The former will always stand for the same ideas and institutions; the meaning of the latter slides on with the times". On this evidence Tyrrell would not have cared much for our contemporary term "post-modern." As Malcolm Bull has put it, "Contrary to Tyrrell's expectations, modernity proved unable to keep up with itself, and modernism has now become as much an absolute as medievalism."[14] That does not affect Tyrrell's argument, since cultural relevance is what he is seeking, whether or not one calls it modernity. His protest is not against medieval theology as such but only against its imposition as an absolute upon the modern Church. He delighted in the thought that St Thomas Aquinas was a thirteenth-century modernist.

Medievalism left Mercier discomfited and wondering whether he should try to answer it himself. The best advice available to him was against any reply. It would, said his advisers, only give Tyrrell more publicity. Wilfrid Ward, while expressing the view that Tyrrell should not be left in possession of the field, believed that Mercier himself should not contest the issue. In the event, Mercier prepared a text but never published it.[15] *Medievalism* was never effectively refuted either at the time or since.

By and large the book was predictably received. Tyrrell was by this time beyond caring about how his enemies would react. He was, however, concerned about the judgment of his friends, especially that of Friedrich von Hügel. He wrote to his Anglican friend, Alfred Lilley, then Vicar of St Mary's, Paddington Green:

> The Baron . . . cited me yesterday *ad audiendum verbum, re Medievalism*. I approached the tribunal like a guilty schoolboy with a half-learnt lesson. Of course, he had it to his fingers' ends; scored, analysed, numbered. To my agreeable surprise he was enthusiastic for every word of it.[16]

The Baron was in point of fact rather more ambivalent than Tyrrell suggests. He constantly tried to moderate his friend's pugnacity and was undoubtedly uncomfortable about the confrontational character of the book. Nevertheless he did pass on to Tyrrell the enthusiastic estimate of "that all-but-unsatisfiable, intensely fastidious Edm. Bishop."[17] This was an endorsement well worth having, for all that it was private. Edmund Bishop, the foremost Catholic liturgical scholar in Britain, kept a very low profile during the modernist crisis. He was happy to describe himself in private as a modernist, but he held the interesting view that the battle for sane Catholicism had been lost forty years earlier when, as he put it to von Hügel in 1913, "the 'faith' that I learnt from the group of English Catholic laymen *wiped out* in the sixties" had now to be somehow kept alive in a Church whose authorities were practising institutional violence and whose members were displaying a consequent pusillanimity.[18] Bishop took heart from *Medievalism* and later told Maude Petre that Tyrrell's "great work was to put in a clear plain unmistakable form what so many persons—may I say conspired?—to blur & confuse. And it cost him his life."[19]

"*Livre de circonstance*," certainly, but also "a work of eloquence, sincerity and faith" was how Loisy, a man not given to the light bestowal of praise in any quarter, described *Medievalism*.[20] Any reader who appreciates lean and lucid prose laced with colourful metaphors, ironic intent and witty instance must surely celebrate this book as a *tour de force* of English prose. Its author uses the English language with precision allied to an instinctive feel for its rhetorical possibilities. The literary form of an open letter offers abundant opportunities for the exercise of those possibilities, and Tyrrell takes them and exploits them with panache. There are rhetorical flourishes here and there that are forensic rather than theatrical, but they are deeply felt and in no way artificially contrived. The reader can delight in the wit, irony and controlled hyperbole without ever losing sight of the case that is being argued. That the biblical references are often in the form of witty allusions rather than of straight quotation gives them added point as well as piquancy. In some respects this book bridges the chasm between reason and feeling, between the Apollonian and the Dionysian, between systematic thought and prophetic protest. Its author is an artist as well as a religious thinker. In fact, it is the strength of his religious convictions that shapes the artistry of his prose style.

"Only a man as outraged *and as religious* as Tyrrell could have written such a work," T. M. Loome has remarked, and it is an important insight into the character of a book which might easily be taken for mere polemic.[21] Many of Tyrrell's friends commented on the mystical side of his temperament, and some of them contrasted it with his polemical side. The contrast is unnecessary: in much of what he wrote the two are of a piece. He had a vision of what the Church should be, and that vision was affronted

17

by the attitudes, actions, and theology of the administrators of the Church of his time. His protest against them was fierce precisely because he made it as an insider and from a position of indignant and disillusioned caring. His agony came about because he could not divorce his care for the Church from his care for truth. If we knew only the circumstances which occasioned *Medievalism*, but not the book itself, we might easily suppose it to have been another minor and ephemeral *apologia*. To read it nearly a century later is to realize that, whatever else it may be, it is neither minor nor ephemeral. The issues it treats of are still large and live in the Church.

Trinity College   *Gabriel Daly*
Dublin

NOTES
1. It was later published, with an introduction, notes and epilogue, under Tyrrell's own name as *A Much-Abused Letter* (London, 1906).
2. N. Sagovsky, *On God's Side: A Life of George Tyrrell* (Oxford, 1990), p. 201.
3. Sagovsky, pp. 197, 199.
4. R. Boudens, "George Tyrrell and Cardinal Mercier: A Contribution to the History of Modernism," *Eglise et Théologie* 1 (1970), p. 316. Boudens' article is especially valuable for its use and generous quotations from Belgian sources, notably the Mercier papers.
5. M. D. Petre, *Autobiography and Life of George Tyrrell*, vol. 2 (London, 1912), p. 504, prints the original Italian text of Ferrata's letter with its controversial phrase "tener corrispondenze epistolari," about the interpretation of which there was substantial disagreement.
6. Boudens, *art. cit.*, pp. 322-3, reproduces the full text of the original letter. It is given in inaccurate and heavily censored form in Petre, *Autobiography and Life*, 2, pp. 304-5.
7. Petre, *Autobiography and Life*, 2, p. 306.

8. Boudens, *art. cit.*, p. 329.

9. *Ibid.*, p. 331.

10. Tyrrell to Petre, 16.3.1905; British Library, Add. MS. 52367.

11. See M. Ward, *Insurrection Versus Resurrection* (London, 1937), pp. 316-7.

12. G. Tyrrell, *Through Scylla and Charybdis: Or, the Old Theology and the New* (London, 1907), pp. 85-105.

13. Tyrrell, *ibid.*, p. 350n. The neologism is "formed from *Theologia*, as sophism is from *Sophia*."

14. M. Bull, "Who Was the First to Make a Pact with the Devil?," *London Review of Books*, vol. 14, n. 9 (14 May 1992), p. 22.

15. It is printed by Boudens as an appendix to his article, pp. 340-51.

16. Tyrrell to Lilley, 8.8.1908; Brit. Lib., Add. MS. 52368.

17. Cited in D. Schultenover, *George Tyrrell: In Search of Catholicism* (Shepherdstown, 1981), p. 341.

18. T. M. Loome has published this important letter in his *Liberal Catholicism, Reform Catholicism, Modernism: A Contribution to a New Orientation in Modernist Research* (Mainz, 1979), pp. 431-6.

19. A. Vidler, *A Variety of Catholic Modernists* (Cambridge, 1970), pp. 150-1.

20. A. Loisy, *Mémoires pour servir à l'histoire religieuse de notre temps*, Vol III, (Paris, 1931), p. 131.

2I. Loome, *Liberal Catholicism*, p.14.

THE LENTEN PASTORAL*

DÉSIRÉ JOSEPH MERCIER, CARDINAL PRIEST OF THE HOLY ROMAN CHURCH; *by the Grace of God and of the Apostolic See* ARCHBISHOP OF MALINES, PRIMATE OF BELGIUM; *to the Clergy and Faithful of our Diocese, health and benediction in our Lord Jesus Christ.*

MOST DEAR BRETHREN,

On the 3rd of July, 1907, the Holy Father caused to be drawn up a catalogue of errors which he condemned, and which later were grouped together under the name of *Modernism*. On the 8th of the following September, in order to explain the reasons underlying this condemnation of Modernism, he gave to the world an Encyclical remarkable for its fulness, clearness and vigour. Thank God, these errors, which have principally taken root in France and Italy, find scarce an adherent in Belgium. Your preservation from them is due to the watchfulness of your Pastors, and to the spirit of scientific impartiality and Christian obedience that animates the representatives of higher education in this country of ours. Nevertheless, My Brethren, I regard it as a duty of my pastoral charge to acquaint you in some measure with this papal Encyclical which will be hereafter known to ecclesiastical history by its opening words: *Pascendi Dominici Gregis*, or more simply by its first word *Pascendi*.

Since the Holy Father addresses his letter to all the particular churches: that is, to the bishops, priests, and laity of the Catholic

---

* There can be little doubt that Tyrrell himself translated Mercier's Lenten Pastoral. Mercier wrote, "La traduction anglaise, que Tyrrell donne de ma lettre pastorale . . . ." [Printed in Boudens, art. cit., p. 341: see n. 4 to Intro. above.] (Ed.)

21

world, he plainly intends that each one should draw profit from it. Moreover, the document is of such importance, and has already attained such historical value, that any one who is interested in the life of the Church should be acquainted with, at least, the substance of its contents. Finally, My Brethren, as soon as the Pope had spoken—nay, before he had spoken, and as soon as the telegrams announced his utterance as imminent —the infidel press set about misrepresenting it. Neither journals nor reviews of the anti-clerical party in this country were honest enough to publish the text, or even the general tenor of the Encyclical; but with an eagerness and unanimity explicable only by party prejudice, they quibbled with the word *Modernism*, and tried to make their credulous readers believe that the Pope had condemned modern thought, which, in their vague language, means modern science and its methods.

This impression, so unjust to the Pope and to those who obey him, has perhaps in all good faith been shared by some of you; in which case we would now undeceive you.

We propose therefore, My Brethren, to speak to you about *Modernism* in order to make you comprehend the motives that have led to its condemnation by the supreme authority of the Church.

What then is Modernism? or rather, since we are not going into details that would interest but few of you, what is the parent-idea or soul of Modernism?

Modernism is not the modern form of science, and therefore the condemnation of Modernism is neither the condemnation of that science of which we are justly so proud, nor the repudiation of its methods which Catholic scientists rightly regard it an honour to put in practice and to teach.

Modernism consists essentially in maintaining that the devout soul should draw the object and motive of its faith from itself and itself alone. It rejects every sort of revealed communication that is imposed on the conscience from outside; and thus, by a necessary consequence, it becomes the denial of the doctrinal authority of the Church established by Jesus Christ, the contempt of the hierarchy divinely appointed to rule the Christian community.

Christ did not come before us as the inventor of a new philosophy, uncertain of himself, committing a body of reformable opinions to the free discussion of his followers. In the strength of his divine wisdom and sovereign power he not only presented to, but imposed upon, men the revealed word which showed them eternal life and the only way to attain it. He proclaimed a moral code for them and gave them the helps necessary to put its prescriptions in practice. Grace, and those sacraments which give it to us, or which restore it to us when, having lost it, we wish to recover it by repentance, constitute the sum-total of these helps—the means of salvation.

He has instituted a Church. As he could be with us only a few years, before leaving us he conferred his powers upon his Apostles to be transmitted to their successors, the Pope and the bishops. The episcopate, in union with the Sovereign Pontiff, has thus received and alone possesses the commission to make known officially and to interpret the doctrines revealed by Christ; it and it alone has the right to condemn with authority all errors inconsistent with those doctrines.

The Christian is one who trusts the teaching of the Church and accepts sincerely the doctrines she proposes for his belief. He who repudiates or questions her authority, and by consequence rejects one or more of the truths she compels him to believe, cuts himself off from the ecclesiastical community.

The excommunication pronounced by the Pope against obstinate Modernists, and which our enemies represent as an act of despotism, is the most simple and natural thing in the world.

My Brethren, we have here merely a question of honesty. Yes or No? Do you believe in the divine authority of the Church? Do you accept exteriorly and interiorly what, in the name of Jesus Christ, she proposes to your belief? Yes or No? Will you consent to obey her?

If yes, then she puts the sacraments at your disposal and undertakes your safe conduct to Heaven.

If no, you deliberately break the bond that united you to her, of which she had tied and blessed the knot. Before God and your conscience you belong to her no more. Do not persist in remaining hypocritically in her midst. Honesty forbids you to pass yourself off any longer as one of her sons; and she who will not and cannot be an accomplice in your sacrilegious hypocrisy requests you, and if necessary summons you, to leave her ranks.

Plainly, however, she rejects you only so long as you yourself will it. The day when, repenting of your error, you return to a loyal recognition of her authority she will welcome you with motherly compassion and with all the affection of the Prodigal's father.

Such then is the constitution of the Catholic Church. The Catholic episcopate, of which the Pope is head, is the heir of the Apostolic College and has authority to instruct the faithful in the Christian revelation.

Just as the head concentrates in itself the life of the entire organism and directs its action in co-ordinating all its movements, so in the same way the Pope ensures the unity of the teaching Church, and every time that there arises a doctrinal dispute among the faithful or the bishops the Pope settles it by an act of his supreme authority. His power is without appeal.

To resume: Each time that a Christian at any moment of his existence asks himself these two important questions:—What should I believe? Why should I believe it? the answer should be: I must believe what is taught me by those Catholic bishops who are in agreement with the Pope; I must believe it because the episcopate united with the Pope is the organ of transmission of the revealed teachings of Jesus Christ.

Be it said, by the way, that the organ of transmission is what is called in one word *Tradition*—to which the belief of the faithful corresponds.

Well then, My Brethren, this Modernism which the Pope has condemned is the denial of just these simple teachings which you learnt in your childhood when you prepared yourselves for your first communion.

The ideas that have given birth to Modernist *doctrines* were sown and fostered in the Protestant soil of Germany and were forthwith transplanted to that of England, and have pushed their shoots as far as the United States.

The Modernist *spirit* has extended to Catholic countries and has given birth to errors on the part of certain writers, forgetful of the Church's tradition, whose enormity alarms the sincere consciences of men simply loyal to the faith of their baptism. This spirit has infected France; Italy has suffered grievously from it; certain English and German Catholics have been affected by it. Belgium is one of the Catholic countries that has best escaped its pernicious influence. You understand, My Brethren, that we are distinguishing between the doctrines of Modernism and the spirit that animates them.

Its doctrines, disseminated in the writings of philosophers, theologians, exegetes or apologists, have been admirably systematised in the Encyclical *Pascendi*; but since you have had the good fortune to escape their infection I will not here trouble myself to show you how they are in contradiction with Faith and with sound philosophy.

But what I more fear for your souls is the contagion of the Modernist spirit. This spirit is the issue of Protestantism. You know what Protestantism is. Luther denied the Church's right to teach the Revelation of Jesus Christ with authority to the Christian community. The Christian, he contends, depends on himself alone for the knowledge of his faith; he derives its elements from the sacred Scriptures which each can interpret directly under the inspiration of the Holy Spirit. He will not allow that there is in the Church an hierarchic authority established to transmit revealed teachings faithfully to the world; to interpret them with full right and assurance, and to guard their integrity unceasingly.

The essential point at issue between Catholicism and Protestantism lies there.

Catholicism says that the Christian Faith is communicated to the faithful by an official organ of transmission—the Catholic episcopate—and that it is based on the acceptance of the authority of that organ. Protestantism on the contrary says that faith is exclusively an affair of individual judgment applied to the interpretation of the Holy Scriptures.

Authority on one side, individualism on the other. A Protestant Church is therefore necessarily invisible; it is the presumed agreement of individual minds as to the same interpretation of Scripture. Protestantism, so formulated, has been condemned by the Council of Trent in the sixteenth century; and there is no longer any one who dares to call himself a Protestant and at the same time to consider himself a Catholic.

But the Protestant *spirit* has leaked here and there into the Catholic conscience and given rise to conceptions in which we find, all at once, piety of intention, the proselytising zeal of a Catholic, and the intellectual aberrations of Protestantism. M. Frederic Paulsen, professor at the rationalistic Protestant university of Berlin, notices this curious fact, *à propos* of the Encyclical *Pascendi*: "It seems clear that all the doctrines condemned by the Encyclical are of German origin, and yet there is perhaps not a single theologian who defends Modernism in the theological Faculties of Germany".*

The observation is significant.

But it is not only today that one finds in the university-world of Germany traces of the Protestant spirit.

When in 1868 Pius IX ordered the assembling of an ecumenical council, Döllinger, an eminent and learned Catholic, professor at the University of Munich, who afterwards openly seceded, wrote, concerning the part played by bishops at such councils: "The bishops should go to the Council to bear witness to the faith of their diocesans; the definitions should give expression to the beliefs of the collectivity."

Notice, My Brethren, already we have the agreement of individual consciences substituted for the rulings of authority.

The most penetrating observer of the present Modernist movement—the one most alive to its tendencies, who has best divined its spirit, and is perhaps more deeply imbued with it than any other, is the English priest Tyrrell.

Now in the numerous works he has published these ten years back we find, besides pages of deep piety (which for our part we have read with profit and a sense of sincere gratitude to the author), we find, often in the spirit that animates these very pages, the fundamental error of Döllinger; that is to say, the parent-idea of Protestantism.

Little wonder, for Tyrrell is a convert whose early education was Protestant.

Ever and almost exclusively attentive to the inward workings of the spirit; little if at all preoccupied with the traditional teachings of dogma or with ecclesiastical history; anxious before all to keep in the Church those of our contemporaries who have been upset by the noisy assertions of unbelievers who, now in the name of natural science, now in that of historical criticism, would pass off their own philosophical prejudices and conjectural hypotheses for assured conclusions of Science in conflict with our faith, Tyrrell, at a distance of forty years, has made a

---

* Internationale Wochenschrift, 7 Dez. 1907.

new attempt analogous to that of the apostate Döllinger.

Revelation, he thinks, is not a deposit of *doctrine* committed to the charge of the teaching Church, and of which the faithful are to receive authoritative interpretation from time to time. It is the *life* of the collectivity of religious souls, or rather, of all men of good will who aspire to realise an ideal higher than the earthly aims of egoists. The Christian saints form the *élite* of this invisible society, this communion of saints. While the *life of religion* pursues its invariable course in the depths of the Christian conscience, *"theological" beliefs* are elaborated by the intellect and find expression in formulae adapted to the needs of the day, but which lose in conformity to the living realities of Faith what they gain in precision. The authority of the Roman Catholic Church —the bishops and the Pope—interprets the interior life of the faithful, recapitulates the results of the general conscience, and proclaims them in dogmatic formulae. But *the interior life of religion remains itself the supreme directive rule of beliefs and dogmas*. In addition, the intellectual effort being subject to a thousand fluctuations, the code of beliefs is variable; and the dogmas of the Church, on their side, change their sense, if not necessarily their expression, with the ages to which they are addressed; still, the Catholic Church remains one and faithful to its beginnings, because, since the time of Christ, one and the same spirit of religion and holiness animates the successive generations of the Christian community, and all agree at bottom in the same sentiment of filial piety towards our Father who is in Heaven and of love for humanity and the universal brotherhood.

Such, my most dear Brethren, is the spirit of Modernism.

The parent-idea of the system has been powerfully influenced by the philosophy of Kant, himself a Protestant and the author of a special theory which opposes the universal certitude of Science to the exclusively personal certitude of the religious sentiment. It has also doubtless been influenced by that infatuation, as general as it is shortsighted, which inclines so many good men to apply, arbitrarily and *a priori*, to history, and especially to the history of our sacred books and dogmatic beliefs, the hypothesis of that evolution which so far from being a general law of human thought, is not even verified in the restricted department of the formation of animal and vegetal species.

27

But in itself the idea, which first inspired many generous champions of Catholic apologetics and caused them to fall into Modernism, is at root identical with that Protestant individualism which is substituted for the Catholic conception of a teaching authority officially established by Jesus Christ, and commissioned to tell us what, under pain of eternal damnation, we are compelled to believe.

This Modernist spirit is in the atmosphere all round us, and it is for this reason no doubt that the Pope, guided specially by Divine Providence, addresses to the Catholics of the whole world an Encyclical whose doctrinal import concerns, it seems, scarcely more than a relatively small fraction of France, England, and Italy.

The *doctrines* repudiated by the Encyclical are such as to shock the Christian conscience by their bare mention. But there is something seductive in the *tendencies* of Modernism; they make an impression on certain minds otherwise loyally attached to the Faith of their Baptism.

Why is this? Why has Modernism such an attraction for youth?

We find two causes for this phenomenon in two quibbles which I wish to expose in the second part of this Pastoral Letter.

The infidel press proclaims loudly that in condemning Modernism the Pope has opposed himself to progress and denied Catholics the right to march with the times. Deceived by this lie, which certain Catholic controversialists have imprudently accredited, some sincere souls, hitherto faithful to the Church, begin to waver and to be discouraged, imagining most erroneously that they cannot at once obey their Christian conscience and serve the cause of scientific advance.

I will make it a matter of duty to answer this calumny of a hostile press in a communication addressed especially to the clergy, of which they may utilise certain extracts for your benefit wherever they think fit.

But is it indeed very necessary to convince men of good faith in Belgium, that in order to be on the Pope's side against Modernism one need not be less with the times in honouring and furthering the progress of science?

Thank God, as we have already said, Belgian Catholics have escaped the heresies of Modernism The representatives of philosophy and theology in our universities and free faculties; and those of the seminaries and religious congregations have unanimously and spontaneously declared and proved in a document signed by each of them that the Pope by his courageous Encyclical has saved the Faith and protected Science.

Now have not these same signatories the right to turn proudly to their accusers and ask them, in the name of those Catholic institutions that they represent: What science is there that we have not served as well, if not better than you? Do our masters fear comparison with yours? Do not the pupils formed by us, when brought to public competition with yours, readily surpass them?

Sacrifice proves the depth of conviction and the sincerity of love. Are you aware, my Brethren, of any generosity on the part of unbelievers to the cause of science? If so, I am glad to hear it, and ask you confidently to compare it with the millions of francs contributed by the generosity of Belgian Catholics to the work of primary, secondary, and higher education.

The second quibble that favours the spread of the spirit of Modernism among the youth, and renders it sometimes attractive to the masses, is the unconscious assimilation of the constitution of the Catholic Church to the political organisations of our modern countries.

Under parliamentary government each citizen is supposed to be invested with a share in public affairs; the revolutionary theories set afloat by J. J. Rousseau and formulated in the Declaration of the Rights of Man (1789) have indoctrinated the masses with the crude idea that the directive authority of a country is the sum of the individual wills of the whole community. The representatives of authority are thus considered as delegates whose exclusive function is to interpret and execute the mind and will of their constituents.

And this is the conception of authority that Döllinger wanted to apply to the bishops united at the Vatican Council. Tyrrell, in his turn, applies it to the bishops as well as to the faithful, lay or ecclesiastic, of the Christian community so as to leave the bishops, and even the Pope, who is the supreme authority, no more than the right of recording and authoritatively proclaiming the thoughts, desires, and feelings of the scattered members of the Christian family, or rather of the communion of religious souls.

29

This analogy, my Brethren, is deceptive. Civil society, following a natural law, springs from the union and co-operation of the wills of its constituent members. But the Church, as a supernatural society, is essentially a positive and external institution, and must be accepted by its members as organised by her Divine Founder. It belongs to Christ Himself to dictate His will to us.

Listen, then, to the supreme and imprescriptible instructions that the Son of God, made man, gives to his apostles: "Go," he bids them, "into the Whole world, and preach the Gospel to all creatures: he who believes the Faith that you teach him and is baptised shall be saved; but he who refuses to believe shall be condemned."

The evangelist S. Mark who quotes these words on the last page of his Gospel concludes his narrative thus: "And the Lord Jesus Christ, after he had thus spoken, was taken up into Heaven and seated at the right hand of God his Father; while the apostles went out in all directions to preach the Gospel with the help of the Lord" (Mark 16:15-20).

Well, then, the bishops continue the apostles' mission. The faithful must hear them, believe their teaching, and obey them under pain of eternal damnation.

If any one refuses to obey the Church, says our Lord again, consider him as a publican and a pagan; that is, as a man who has no faith (cf. Matt. 18:17). For "Verily I say to you whatsoever you shall bind on earth shall be bound in Heaven, and whatsoever you shall loose on earth shall be loosed in Heaven" (Matt. 18:18).

CONCLUSION

Cling, my Brethren, to the corner-stone of your Faith. Depend on your bishop, who himself depends on the successor of Peter, the bishop of bishops, the immediate representative of the Son of God, our Lord Jesus Christ.

Watch vigilantly over the treasure of your Faith, without which no other possession, no sort of good work will profit you for eternity.

Perfect yourselves in religious instruction.

My Brethren, [it is]* not astonishing that, as a young man

---

* Original has "is it" (Ed.).

grows up, he takes a pride in developing his bodily strength, in adding to the amount of his knowledge, in forming his judgment, in deepening his experience, in improving his speech, in refining his style, in mastering the ways of the world, in keeping in touch with the course of events. Every man takes his professional studies to heart. Tell me, where is the lawyer, magistrate, physician, or merchant who at the age of forty would not be ashamed to own that he had learnt nothing new since he was twenty?

Now is it not true that many a Catholic of twenty, thirty, or forty years would, if asked, be forced to confess that since his first communion he had learnt nothing, and perhaps forgotten a good deal, of his religion?

I understand that in this period of confusion irreligion should make conquests; and I deplore the fact. But what I less understand is that an intelligent believer, conscious of the favour God has conferred upon him with the privilege of Faith, should be content not to know what he believes, or why he believes it, or to what duties towards God and man his solemn baptismal promises bind him.

Every educated man ought to have a catechism in his library, if not to commit it anew to memory, at least to meditate on the text. The best catechism is that of the *Council of Trent* with its marvellous clearness, precision, and method, in which, by order of the Fathers of that Council, a commission of competent theologians has condensed the substance of Faith, and Morality, and Christian institutions.

To learn the object of their Faith, educated Catholics ought moreover to possess a manual of the Church's dogmatic teachings (such as Denzinger's) and the chief papal encyclicals addressed to our generation, especially those of Leo XIII of glorious memory, and of His Holiness Pius X.

Then they ought to have at hand, if not the whole text of the Bible, at least the *New Testament*; that is to say, the Gospels, the apostolic epistles, and the narrative of the Acts of the Apostles. They ought also to have a *History of the Church* and an *Apologetic Treatise*.

To interest and foster his piety, every man should possess the *Roman Missal* and a *Treatise on Liturgy* to explain to him the ceremonies of the Mass and the chief rites of the Church's religious worship.

The *Imitation of Christ*, Bossuet's *Meditations on the Gospel*, the *Devout Life* of S. Francis of Sales, together with some saints' lives to show us the Gospel in action, would, taken together, furnish, at a very moderate price, the minimum of a religious library for a Christian family.

Every family, however humble, should possess some books on religion and piety. We shall shortly give more definite information on this subject, here but touched on, for the benefit of French and Flemish readers.

I have sometimes run my eye over the libraries of friends devoted to the liberal professions; I have found works on science, literature, and secular history; but how often have I sought in vain for a shelf of religious literature!

Is it very wonderful that a boldly formulated difficulty should easily get hold of minds so ill-equipped for resistance? Then they get alarmed and turn for aid to apologetic.

Doubtless apologetic has its uses in the Church. Attacks call for defence. Sick men send for the doctor But hygiene is better than physic. Study rather the explanations and proofs of Catholic doctrine; saturate your minds with its teachings; acquaint yourselves with the history of the Church; inform yourselves about the labours of her apostolate.

After that: Watch and pray. By the integrity of your lives, the purity of your morals, by the humble acknowledgment of your need of God and his Providence, repress the self-interested reasonings of unbelief and you will, as often as not, see the doubts that rise in your mind and obscure its outlook dispersed like clouds before the light of the sun. And if now and then a doubt on some special point occurs to you, consult a treatise on apologetic; or better still, seek an enlightened guide; for the solution you shall thus receive will be suited to your particular mentality and momentary requirements; it will be far more useful than one addressed indefinitely to a large public of readers or hearers at once.

My dear Brethren, in reality we do not sufficiently appreciate the blessings of Faith. Man is so constituted that he ceases to notice what is habitual. How often do you thank God for your good sight or hearing; for sound lungs and heart? Were you threatened with the loss of them, you would at once realise their value and be keenly grateful for their restoration.

My Brethren, the Protestant nations are sick. The potion of free enquiry has been working on them for now four centuries. Observe how religious souls are harassed by the thousand and one sects who clamour for their adhesion without any title for their special claim.

I remember an Anglican minister who was converted to Catholicism about 1895. With his characteristic straightforwardness he taught his parishioners the Divinity of Jesus Christ as he himself believed it. A fellow-minister, pastor of a neighbouring parish, denied the same openly in the presence of his flock. The devout population, in dismay, asked for a solution of the controversy. The bishop of the two parishes stood up for the Godhead of Christ, but was notoriously disavowed by his archbishop. What guidance can such confusion afford? Is it conceivable that we should be obliged to believe the Gospel, and that there is no one qualified to tell us its meaning?

The Anglican minister, whom I remember very distinctly, could not bring himself to think so. Social unity of Faith is impossible without authority; authority in the matter of Faith is incomplete without the privilege of infallibility. Thus he said and thus he believed. He recognised the authority of the Pope, and became, in his turn, an apostle of the Roman and Catholic Faith.

And it is at this moment, when religious Protestants, harassed by liberalism and tossed with doubt, are crying out in despair for the help of authority, and saying: "Lord, save us: we perish!" that Modernists would rob us of that Head which the sectaries envy us, and would ask us to make again that experiment whose failure has been proved by four miserable centuries.

No, my dearest Brethren, let us not repeat that wretched experience. Let us gather more closely than ever round Peter, the Vicar of Jesus Christ. The unity of the Christian Faith is saved only in the Catholic Church; the Catholic Church is firm only on the throne of Peter. "We will turn, therefore," said S. Irenaeus, bishop of Lyons at the end of the second century, "towards the greatest and oldest of the Churches, known to all, the Church founded and established at Rome by the two glorious apostles Peter and Paul; we will show that the tradition which she holds from the apostles and the Faith which she proclaims to men have reached us through the regular succession of her bishops; and this will put to confusion all those who whether through vanity, or blindness, or evil desire, take up indiscriminately with any opinion that pleases them. For such is the superiority and pre-eminence of the Church of Rome that all the Churches—that is to say, the faithful from all parts of the globe—ought to be in agreement with her; and that in her, believers, whencesoever they come, find the apostolic tradition intact."*

[Here follows the Lenten Indult.]

The present Pastoral Letter and the Lenten Indult that follows it, shall be read in the pulpit in the Churches, public chapels, religious communities and colleges of the diocese. They shall be posted up there, and so remain till the end of Lent.

Given at Malines, etc.,
✠D. J. CARDINAL MERCIER, etc.

---

* Adv. Haer. III.3.

MEDIEVALISM

A REPLY TO CARDINAL MERCIER

Your Eminence,—

Since you have thought fit to mention me by name in your Lenten Pastoral (1908) as the most typical embodiment of the Modernism which you are there denouncing; since you profess to draw your description of that movement from my writings; since your Pastoral has received the special commendation of the Holy Father; and since you have now chosen to give it the permanent and wider publicity of a brochure, you can hardly wonder if I assert the inalienable right of every man to speak in the defence of what he believes to be the truth.

For many reasons, I confess, Your Eminence's action has surprised me. I have certainly no claim of friendship to urge against one with whom I have never had any direct communications; but our indirect communications, initiated two years ago by Your Eminence, were certainly not unfriendly. That the steps which you then took in my behalf were the occasion of all my subsequent ecclesiastical difficulties was surely not due to lack of good will on your part, but to the machinations of others. Still it was a reason for thinking that Your Eminence would be the last bishop who would willingly add to those difficulties of which you had been the innocent occasion, or who would do anything to complicate an all but hopeless situation. Is there not something in the Gospel about "the bruised reed" and "the smoking flax"? Was any man ever yet made better by being pilloried before the world? Even the Encyclical *Pascendi*, which does not err on the side of excessive tenderness and charity, is content to signalise errors without mentioning names. Is it not enough to be as zealous as the Pope?

Possibly it is that same Encyclical which has led you to look upon your past kindliness as an indiscretion, as something to be repudiated and explained away. In that case you will welcome this reply as proving that your sympathies were due to a complete misunderstanding; and as exonerating you from the slightest complicity with Modernism.

I am not ashamed of "Modernism." When you speak of me as "the most penetrating observer of contemporary Modernism . . . the man most profoundly imbued with its spirit," I should feel flattered were I coxcomb enough to believe myself level with those leaders of the movement whom I follow, from whom I have learnt everything, and from whom I have yet so much to learn. But, for Your Eminence, Modernism is the deadliest of heresies, and heresy the deadliest moral obliquity; and of this obliquity you present me, first to Belgium, and now to the world, as the most deeply imbued representative. Seeing it was quite unnecessary, I can hardly think it was friendly, or even charitable, to take such uncalled-for action, which would have come much better from the Archbishop of Westminster. It is in England and not in Belgium that I am known and read.

Again, you are good enough to say that you owe me a debt of gratitude for some things I have written in those very pages which you describe as "animated with the fundamental error of Döllinger and the parent-idea of Protestantism." It is no doubt a light debt, but heavy enough to have turned a more delicate balance in my favour; nor could I have imagined that, when some years ago I trustingly put one of my suppressed books *Oil and Wine* into what I supposed were your sympathetic hands,

I was supplying a weapon to be used against myself later.

And finally, Your Eminence is aware of the recent censures declared against those who speak and write in favour of Modernism or Modernists, or against the Encyclical *Pascendi*. Is it quite generous to assail men by name who can defend themselves only by what you consider a rebellion against legitimate authority—to strike those who are bound hand and foot? If you foresee such rebellion are you not responsible for it? If not, do you not take advantage of your adversary's helplessness? Or is it noble to attack me before a public whom you can forbid to read my reply should it prove inconvenient?

These are the reasons why I was surprised and, I must say, disappointed to find myself pilloried in Your Eminence's Lenten Pastoral.

But there were other surprises of a more important and less personal description. I had long heard of Your Eminence as a man of general culture, in sympathy with the intellectual needs of the day. True, your special interest had been in the scholastic revival at Louvain. But unlike the neo-scholasticism at Rome, that at Louvain seeks honestly to reconcile itself with the results and methods of science and to patch the new cloth of contemporary culture on to the old medieval garment; and this laudable endeavour has been (I am told) in great measure due to the encouragement and inspiration of Your Eminence.

When, therefore, I heard of your elevation to the Cardinalate my first feeling was one of sincere regret. For the nearer one draws to the centre, and the further from the circumference, of the official Church, the tighter and heavier are the fetters imposed on one's mental and moral liberty; and the harder it is to realise one's own personality. Whence the Roman adage: *Promoveatur ut amoveatur.** Still it was some consolation to know that in the ranks of

---

* "Let him be promoted in order to remove him" (Ed.).

the Sacred College there would now be at least one man in intelligent sympathy with the mental exigencies of the times and capable of moderating the extravagances of ignorance and fanaticism.

So far as Your Eminence's Pastoral Letter is an unfettered expression of your own personal convictions, and not merely a dutiful conformity to the ideas and sentiments of the Encyclical *Pascendi*, I must own that my sanguine anticipations were ungrounded. It is true that in your estimate of the constitution of the Church; of the scope and meaning of the Gospel; of my own aims and endeavours, I seem to see a certain inconsistency—a conflict as it were between a broader and a narrower spirit. But there is no doubt as to which is the conqueror and which the conquered, or as to the ascendency of the official view over the personal—of obedience over inclination.

Permit me then to make a few comments on the text of your Pastoral Letter.

I

THE IMMUNITY OF BELGIUM

YOU begin by thanking God "that the errors which have spread over France and Italy have found almost no advocates in Belgium," and this happy state of things you ascribe to "the vigilance of the Pastors; to the scientific impartiality and Christian obedience of the teachers"—a reflection not quite complimentary to the French and Italian episcopate.

Your Eminence, if the consensus of the bishops were valid against the assurance of the Pope, one would easily believe that there were no such movement in the world as Modernism. For Germany has been pronounced unspotted by the Holy Father himself; England declared guiltless by the Archbishop of Westminster; the Americans affirm that it is an exclusively European malady; the Italians say that the Encyclical was intended for France; the French, that it was clearly aimed at Italy. Every bishop thanks God that his diocese has been preserved as an oasis of light in the desert of Egyptian darkness; each asks: Is it I? none confesses: It is I.

But in default of actual knowledge, I am quite willing to believe that Belgium is exceptionally, if not wholly, free from the disease; not precisely owing to the causes which you assign, but to others which you mention, though not recognising them as causes.

The picture which Your Eminence gives, in the *Conclusion* of your Pastoral Letter, of the sad lack of interest in the subject of religion on the part of educated Belgians is not quite in harmony with the cheerful note that opens your discourse; and by no means so eloquent a testimony to the vigilance of religious pastors and teachers. You complain that "whereas lawyers, magistrates, doctors and merchants would be ashamed to own at forty that their professional knowledge was no greater than twenty years ago, educated Catholics of the same age are not ashamed to have learnt nothing about their religion since their first communion."

You say that you have often sought in vain for "a shelf of religious literature" in the well-stored libraries of your cultivated Catholic friends. You speak of the "conquests made by irreligion" and ascribe them to this same lack of religious interest and knowledge. You suggest, amongst other books for the "religious shelf," the Catechism, the Bible, or at least the New Testament (whose contents you think it necessary to enumerate—as it were for pagans), the Roman Missal, the Imitation of Christ. Could any one who knows England imagine an Anglican bishop urging the educated or even uneducated members of his flock to possess themselves of the Bible and the Book of Common Prayer? Does Your Eminence suppose that in those three great Protestant countries—England, Germany, and America—whose spiritual sickness you deplore (*"les nations protestantes sont malades"*) and to whose influence you trace the malaria of Modernism, there is a single Christian household without its Bible and its devotional literature? Have you ever had the curiosity to contrast the annual output of religious literature of a Protestant country like Germany or England, with that of a Catholic country like Spain or Ireland? Have you ever had the opportunity of observing the keen and universal interest in religious questions in countries where the laity still count for something in the life of the Church? If there are two Catholic countries in which the output of religious literature today marks a revival of religious interest, they are just the two which you describe as the centres of Modernism—France and Italy. And why is this?

It is because when you have made a desert, you call it peace; it is because you mistake the quiet of Death for the quiet of Life; the stillness of silence, for the stillness of harmony; the poverty of uniformity, for the richness of organic unity.

I am not blind to the fact that variety without unity may be almost as great an evil as unity without variety; that where general agreement is not the goal of all individual effort, and where diversity is accepted as final and satisfactory, there can be no progress, but only an aimless analysis and disintegration. It is for that reason that we need an institutional Church within whose boundary-walls all these varieties of individual experience and reflection are pressed together and forced to seek a synthesis sooner or later. For thus only do they become fruitful for the general advantage. But the military uniformity of a multitude whose duty is to have no ideas of their own, but to accept those of their commander, as wax accepts the impression of a seal, has nothing whatever to do with spiritual unity, and can only result in that utter absence of interest in religious subjects which you observe in the otherwise cultivated and intelligent members of your flock. I say "otherwise" cultivated; for I do not see how he can be called simply a cultivated man who is dead to the deepest and most universal of rational interests—that which unifies and embraces all the rest. It is just the lack of all response to this interest that renders the converse of the typical ultramontane layman and even of the typical ultramontane priest so profoundly uninteresting and devitalising. Touch on this subject and he looks at you with the stone eyes of a statue.

How could it be otherwise? Tell the layman, as the Encyclical does, that his religious thought in no way contributes to the penetration and better understanding of the Christian faith; that he has no business to meddle with or investigate a subject which is the exclusive concern of the episcopate; or rather, of the Pope; tell him, moreover, that there can be no real progress in religious knowledge; that the fulness of Catholic truth was stereotyped once and for all two thousand years ago, and is stored up in the secret archives of the Vatican; that uncertainties are to be solved not by mental struggle, but by a simple reference to those archives; tell him all this, and why, in Heaven's name, should he trouble his head about religion any more than about the further developments of the multiplication table? By the time we have got from twice two to twelve times twelve our interest is dead. We know the trick, and how to find twenty times twenty if necessary.

Your Eminence is, I believe, a psychologist. You must then know that what is absolutely simple is absolutely uninteresting; that thought is essentially a movement of enquiry—of asking, seeking, knocking. "The lawyer, the magistrate, the doctor, the merchant" all know that by their independent thought and ingenuity they can further the general progress of their professional interests; that there is always more to be known and discovered. But the Catholic is taught at the time of his first communion that there is no progress to be made in religious knowledge, and that if there were, he has no active concern in the matter. Nor is the priest here in a better condition than the layman; nay, the very bishops have no longer any other duty than to sit still and listen to the Pope—to the one and only active principle of ecclesiastical life before whom bishops, priests, and laymen are passive as clay in the hands of the potter, or as dumb sheep in the hands of the shearer.

Of the two evils, such a sterilising uniformity seems to me far greater than the divisions and subdivisions of Protestantism. These, at least, are evidences of energy and vitality, however wasted for lack of the unifying pressure of rational authority. Here are people who live and feel and think their religion; who are interested enough to quarrel about it, as about the most vital of all questions. Here, at least, is a variety out of which it is possible to make a unity. But from a mechanical uniformity, secured by the discouragement and repression of individual interest and initiative, what can result but that which has resulted?

By regimental drill, by governmental coercion, you may form a political party, you may drive the multitudes to Mass and to the Sacraments, you may teach them the same formulas, you may scare them into obedience, you may make them wheels in a machine, but you will never make them living members of a living organism; you will never wake their intelligent interest or enlist their profoundest enthusiasm.

The lowest degree of truly spontaneous and independent spiritual unity, such as obtains in the Anglican Church, or even between the different Protestant sects, is infinitely more significant, strong and durable than the merely artificial and external uniformity to which you trust for the preservation of the Church and the Catholic religion. In spite of all their theological heresies and divisions, the religious interest still lives and grows in Protestant countries, whereas it languishes and dies among Catholics under this modern craze for centralisation and military uniformity.

What could be more admirably drilled than was the French Church under Napoleon III?* What was it all worth in the day of trial and temptation when everything depended on an intelligent laity, spontaneously interested in their religion, and regarding it as their own concern and not merely as a clerical monopoly?

Your Eminence, if there is as little educated interest in

---

*Napoleon III, more commonly known as Louis Napoléon, Emperor of the French, 1852-70, drew heavily on right-wing clerical support and in return favoured French ultramontanism. He also sent troops to fight for Pope Pius IX in the latter's struggle to retain the Papal States (Ed.).

religion among your flock as you say, if men are unaffected by New Testament criticism only because they have never read the New Testament, believe me the history of the French Church will soon repeat itself in Belgium—"Ye shall all likewise perish."

If, then, there is no Modernism in Belgium it may just possibly be because there is so little educated interest in religion among the younger laity and clergy; because they do not know enough or care enough about it to feel the necessity of bringing it into unity with the rest of their thought and knowledge; and because they never try to translate into living ideas, sacred formulae which it is a duty to repeat, an irreverence to examine. Granted for the moment that Modernism is pure heresy, yet its presence in France and Italy is a symptom of reawakened religious interest; and where there is interest there is life and consequently hope. It may be at least the weed that indicates a fertile soil.

Your Eminence, we should thank God for all His mercies; but the absence of Modernism from Belgian soil may perhaps be a very small mercy; and the absence of religious interest a very ominous symptom of approaching exhaustion and sterility. Is it not much worse to have to acknowledge, instead of Modernism, the existence of a "hostile press"; of growing irreligiousness; of a strong anti-clerical liberalism that competes with you for the ascendency in political and educational influence? This is no invasion from outside, but a movement fed by defections from within, and provoked by the very evils that Modernism seeks to mitigate and remedy—by an utter disbelief in that divine purpose which guides the onward and upward struggle of humanity outside as well as inside the Church.

II

THE SUPPOSED ESSENCE OF MODERNISM

B Y way, therefore, of preserving your flock from a corruption which so far has left them untainted, Your Eminence proceeds to explain to them the very essence, "the soul," "the parent-idea" of Modernism. You begin by saying that "Modernism is not the modern expression of science." Nothing more certain. And at once you infer that "consequently the condemnation of Modernism is not the condemnation of science and its methods." The inference is illogical. For though Modernism is more than modern science, it implies and includes an acceptance of the methods and results of that science. Whether or not these are implicitly condemned we shall see later (page 114).

Next you proceed to tell us that "Modernism consists essentially in affirming that the devout soul should derive the object and motive of its Faith from itself and from itself alone. It rejects every sort of revealed communication imposed upon the conscience from outside; and so by a necessary consequence it becomes the denial of the doctrinal authority of the Church established by Jesus Christ, the contempt of the hierarchy divinely appointed to rule the Christian community."

Your Eminence, will you allow one whom you too flatteringly describe as "the most penetrating observer of contemporary Modernism" to qualify the above definition as a most astounding and paradoxical misrepresentation? It is the statement of one who has either never studied the works of a single representative Modernist; or else has read them so hastily and superficially as to be unqualified to pass judgment in the matter. Every single clause of the statement is the direct opposite of the truth. Moreover, it is in flagrant contradiction with the very inadequate description you give of my own position a few pages later.

For there you show how, according to me, Catholic truth is elaborated by the collective religious experience and reflection of the whole Church; how it is interpreted, formulated and imposed by the official hierarchy. We have thus a body of doctrine of which the Church is the organ and guardian; which no single individual has elaborated out of his own conscience; which is presented to his belief from outside; which possesses all the authority of the collective mind over the individual mind. And in the face of this you can describe us as pure individualists; each deriving the motive and object of his Faith from his own spirit, denying all external teaching, all hierarchic authority. You present as the extremest form of Protestantism what is essentially the Catholic conception of religion as a collective life and thought and sentiment—in a word, as a tradition.

Is it that Your Eminence felt in duty bound first to repeat unwillingly but with blind obedience the travesties of the Encyclical *Pascendi* for the edification of your flock and to stir them up against those men whose adhesion to the Church you had to describe as a "sacrilegious hypocrisy"; and that, having fulfilled this disagreeable duty, you thought you might then make a little quiet sacrifice to Charity and Justice, and let them see that even the most typical Modernist was not such an imbecile as to cling to the Church while denying the necessity of a Church? Such was my first explanation of the extraordinary discrepancy between your definition of Modernism and your present-ment of my position. But the real explanation does less credit to Your Eminence's penetration and judgment. The truth is that you do not see the discrepancy in question. Having described how I substitute a spiritual for a mechanical conception of the mode of revelation—which is by no means the same as denying an external revelation— you sum up my position thus: "The authority of the Roman Catholic Church—the bishops and the Pope— interprets the inner life of the faithful, gathers up the results of the collective conscience, and proclaims them in dogmatic formulae. *But the interior religious life itself remains the supreme criterion of beliefs and dogmas.*"

By underlining these words you plainly intend to convict me of the pure individualism described in your formal definition of Modernism. You suppose that I make the individual, and not the collective, religious life the source and criterion of dogmatic truth. You do not see that such an interpretation of the underlined words makes blank nonsense of those that precede; which, therefore, you have strung together without any true idea of their connection or bearing. And since you imply that you are acquainted with my writings, you must have read them to singularly little purpose not to know that my consistent aim from first to last has been to defend the Catholic principle, *"securus judicat orbis terrarum,"* against every sort of individualism—whether that which makes each man's private judgment its own rule, or that which imposes the private judgment of one upon all the rest.

The aim of the theological party in which Your Eminence trusts so implicitly is to persuade the uneducated and half-educated multitudes that there is no choice but of one or other of these individualisms; that those who refuse the new-fangled dictatorial conception of the papacy—i.e. of a privileged private judgment to which all must submit—have no alternative but absolute self-suffciency.

The alternative, Your Eminence, is Catholicism, the subjection of the private and individual to the public and collective mind of the Church. But you were bound to show that I must be a Protestant, since I am not an ultramontane; and so you underline words which out of their context might perhaps bear a Protestant sense, but which, where they stand, could have only one possible meaning for an unbiassed intelligence. That the religious life of the Church is the source and criterion of doctrinal truth; that experiment is the criterion of theory as the fruit is of the tree, is a point that I will not even discuss. It is a truth that theological pride hates and kicks against, but which it dares not deny in the teeth of the Gospel or merely in the name of a discredited knowledge-theory.

III

THE SUPPOSED ESSENCE OF
CATHOLICISM

AND now having presented Modernism as the purest, so-called "Protestant" individualism, and as the repudiation of a divinely established hierarchic Church with authority to teach and rule, your Pastoral goes on to develop that individualistic conception of papal authority which you would persuade your readers is the only possible or actual alternative. Because Modernists repudiate this unhistorical latter-day ultramontanism you pretend they must necessarily be Protestants pure and simple.

Before going further, I would ask you a plain straightforward question. There are about one hundred million Christians of the several Eastern Churches whose fault is an all too rigid adherence to the traditions of the past; who perpetuate, with the fidelity of a stone monument, the beliefs of the early centuries; who hold to the same creeds, the same sacraments, the same priesthood as do their Western brethren. Are they pure individualists? Do they deny the need and existence of a teaching Church? And yet do they not repudiate your modern interpretation of the papacy as an heretical and fantastic innovation unknown to antiquity? Is the Greek Church Protestant?

You will hardly like to attribute such a venerable antiquity to Protestantism, and yet you will have to do so. For you quote as "the fundamental error of Döllinger" and as "the mother-idea of Protestantism" his words: "The bishops should go to the Council to testify to the faith of their diocesans, and the definitions should be the expression of the beliefs of the collectivity."

That, Your Eminence, is the unbroken and universal tradition of the Eastern Churches; nay, even the Roman Church has not yet dared to deny it. And you call this Protestantism and Individualism! Your Eminence's vocabulary is surely somewhat bewildering! Modernists can hardly be surprised to find themselves dubbed Protestants by one who can accuse Dr. Döllinger and the Eastern Churches of individualism in religion. It can only be that absorption in the problems of scholasticism has left Your Eminence no sufficient leisure to study this chapter of the history of dogma.

It is to the Catechism you go for your Church-theory: "Let us call to mind the teachings of the Catechism on the constitution and mission of the Catholic Church." It is a more expeditious source of information than the traditions of the Church, the Fathers, the Councils, the history of dogma. But is it so sure? Have not the popular catechisms, together with the seminary manuals, of these two past generations been carefully revised and re-edited in the interests of a particular interpretation of the Vatican Council and to exclude the only one that can save the Roman Church from the imputation of heresy and apostasy? Are they not the work of that faction of absolutists which strove all but triumphantly, in 1870, to destroy the constitution of the Church; to make ornamental nonentities of the bishops; and to substitute, as the rule of faith, the private judgment of the Pope instead of the public judgment of the whole Church as represented by the entire episcopate ?

At the beginning of the last century the Catholics of England and Ireland read in their approved Catechism (Keenan's Catechism) that the doctrine of papal infallibility was the invention of Protestant calumniators. Catechisms, therefore, are not a very safe rule of faith.

The Church-theory of these recent catechisms is exceedingly simple—dangerously and meretriciously simple. We all know it. In these days when the tares of the heresy have declared their nature so unmistakably and when bishops are groaning under the practical bondage brought upon them by their easy and obsequious compliance in 1870, it is more possible to trace their roots back into the past. It is easy to see how, at a time when men knew nothing of the Church's past and were destitute of the historico-critical sense, it was possible to elaborate and gain credit for such a theory on the strength of very worthless *a priori* reasons, supported by half a dozen misinterpreted texts of Scripture and by a whole body of forged decretals. It is easy to see how such a Church-theory was needed to justify the contested claims of a Church which, not content with its lawful precedence, desired to gather the spiritual power of all the other Churches into its own hands and so to bring the whole world under its own rule and to use that absolute spiritual power as a weapon of universal domination. Without such a spiritual claim the domination of the medieval papal monarchy had been impossible. And to this crude simplification S. Thomas Aquinas, duped by the false decretals and ignorant of history and of the need of history, lent the support of his most deservedly great name. We know how the Court of Rome has clung to it, and by what methods it has been fostered and furthered; how the Society of Jesus has lived for its service and after three centuries nearly forced it upon the Vatican Council; how that Society still works hand in hand with the Curialists to secure the complete obliteration of the ancient Catholic principle which sees in the Pope merely the witness to and the representative of the collective mind and will of the Universal Church; which holds his utterances as *ex cathedra* only when he speaks in that capacity—only when it is manifestly the whole body which speaks to us through that particular organ.

You begin your exposition of the Catechism most admirably by telling us that Christ did not come to found a philosophical school or to deliver the world over to interminable disputations; that he came to reveal to us eternal life and the way to attain it; that "He promulgated a code of morality and gave us the means to put it in practice;" that "grace and the sacraments . . . constitute the sum total of these means, the entire economy of salvation." Nothing could be more true, more evangelical. The Kingdom of Heaven and the means to attain it; the ideal and the dynamic—that is the whole Gospel. Would to Heaven they would take it to heart who try to turn the Church into a school of subtle disputations; who confound revelation with theology, faith with theological orthodoxy; who would drive men out of the Church and into eternal perdition over problems that transcend the wit of man, and have no conceivable bearing on the spiritual life; who attach salvation to formulae which they themselves do not understand, and which, examined closely, are found absolutely void of any intelligible meaning. Would that you yourself held consistently to this summary of Christianity and did not take away with one hand what you have given with the other. But it is too evident that you regard the Church as commissioned, not to preach the Gospel like her Master, but to teach theological science, which her Master never did. Twice you insist, and with a gusto that reminds one of Tertullian, that we must accept theological definitions, as such, and as distinct from the revelation which they protect, "under pain of eternal damnation." I say nothing as to the dubious authenticity of the text which you quote in support of this most un-Christlike sentiment; but your exegesis is somewhat uncritical and fantastic.

"Go into all the world and preach the Gospel to every living creature. He that believeth (the faith which you teach) and is baptised shall be saved, and he that believeth not shall be condemned" (Mark 16:15).

The words I have put in parentheses are, I think, Your Eminence's private gloss, for I cannot find this reading anywhere. I do not object to them; though I have no doubt that by "faith" you mean, and intend your readers to understand, correct theology. But can you seriously think that "Preach the Gospel" means "Teach theology"?

Does it not mean that the Apostles are to do what Christ did? Do you find Christ, in this same Gospel of S. Mark, imposing theological definitions "under pain of eternal damnation"? "The time is accomplished; the Kingdom of God is at hand; repent and believe the good news" is the sum and substance of his preaching. He has no entirely new doctrine about the nature of the Kingdom of Heaven, nor as to the meaning of repentance. He but imparts a new life, a more spiritual tone to very simple ideas already current among his hearers. His work was to kindle the cold hearts and strengthen the faltering wills of those who knew the way right well but could not, or would not, walk in it; it was the work of a preacher or prophet, and not of a theologian. And so when he says "He that believeth and is baptised shall be saved, and he that believeth not shall be condemned," he simply means that those who believe that the Kingdom is at hand, who "repent and are baptised for the remission of their sins" (Acts 2:38), shall enter into that Kingdom; while those who do not shall be left outside the Ark of Salvation in the day of the general Deluge.

Your Eminence's reference to Matthew 18:17 is not much more felicitous. Our Lord is there shown to us as founding the custom of the primitive, but already decadent, Church, by which Christians were forbidden to carry their litigations before pagan judges or to scandalise the world by their internal dissensions. If two believers could not agree together nor accept the arbitration of a neighbour, the affair was to be decided by the religious community. If they refused the judgment of the community and appealed to the profane courts, they were guilty of schism and became as outsiders—as heathens and publicans. There is not in this text even the shadowiest support for the notion of a Church imposing theological definitions "under pain of eternal damnation." Did Christ, the friend of heathens and publicans, consign the heathens and publicans to eternal flames for their heterodoxy? Did he, like Tertullian, revel in the prospect of seeing unbelievers punished in the torments of hell? None dare say so; and if any think so "they know not of whose spirit they are"—the spirit of the unconverted Boanerges; of those who have hated, burnt, and tortured their fellow Christians in the proud empty name of theological orthodoxy. No, Your Eminence, no man has ever yet been saved or lost by theology since the world began: men have been lost for desiring and, as far as was in their power, procuring the excommunication, the temporal and spiritual perdition of their neighbours; for destroying with their theology the souls for whom Christ died.

If you had followed my writings at all carefully you would know that I believe firmly in the necessity and utility of theology; but of a living theology that continually proceeds from and returns to that experience of which it is the ever tentative and perfectible analysis. The simplest and most elementary religious experience involves some theological thought and imagery. What I deny is a theology that draws ideas from ideas, instead of from experience; that gives us shadows of shadows instead of shadows of reality; that wanders further and further from facts along the path of curious and unverified deductions; that makes itself the tyrant instead of the servant of religious life; that imposes its conclusions as divinely revealed, and "under pain of eternal damnation." It was his defiance of such a theology that cost Christ his life at the hands of the "Curialists" of Jerusalem. What I affirm is that those who follow Christ as the Way and the Life, who accept and practise "the moral code which he has promulgated," accept implicitly the full measure of theology necessary for salvation. To make that theology explicit, to deduce its intellectual consequences, is useful for the community as a whole; but to bind this explicit theology on the conscience of each and all, to demand more than the implicit acceptance involved in Christian life and practice, is to set a stumbling-block in the path of salvation. Were it not for this tyranny the whole world would be Christian today. After all, S. Mark believed that his little book contained all that was really necessary for a Christian to know for his salvation. He was not consciously contributing to the volume called the New Testament, or depending on the supplementary matter of S. Paul or of the other evangelists. Yet you will look in vain for any explicit theology in his presentment of the Gospel. If such explicitness was not necessary then, when did it become necessary, and who had authority to make salvation more difficult than Christ made it?

If I insist so much on this point, it is because your conception of the teaching authority of the episcopate and the Pope rests on the false assumption that Christ came primarily as a teacher of correct theology; that, when he prayed (John 17) that his Church might be one, he was not putting mutual charity before us as the distant goal of our prayers and efforts, but was promising us an immediate and perpetual theological uniformity. For the solution of theological controversies it is quite evident that the collective mind of the whole community is a slow and cumbrous instrument. It moves no quicker in theology than it does in any other science, but blunders on through all sorts of errors and excesses till it stumbles at last upon a more approximate truth. Even if we exclude the laity and lower clergy from all competence and participation in the process, yet the united episcopate is for that purpose hardly more expeditious; and the machinery of ecumenical councils works far too slowly and laboriously.

Plainly the "simplest" plan to secure theological unity is to refer matters to one infallible theologian —the Pope— who can settle every question and enforce uniformity at a

moment's notice. Since such an expedient is alone sufficient to secure theological unity it is plain that Christ
ought to, and therefore must, have so arranged matters;
and there is more than one ambiguous text in support of
this *a priori* demonstration.

But, Your Eminence, if Christ had intended and provided for such theological uniformity, how do you account for the long and bitter ante-Nicene controversies
about the Blessed Trinity, the Hypostatic Union, the personality of the Holy Spirit, i.e. about the most central
doctrines of our theology? How came it that generations
of Christians lived holily and died happily ignoring or
denying points that were only settled by some ecumenical
council after perhaps centuries of uncertainty; or that SS
Augustine and Bernard and Thomas Aquinas rejected the
Immaculate Conception, which was a debated point till
1854? If certainty was so vitally necessary why was it
withheld so long? Why should men of today be forced to
believe "under pain of eternal damnation" what S. Thomas
and S. Bernard denied with impunity?

And more especially, if your reading of the Vatican
Decrees is right; if the Popes, independently of the episcopate and the Church, have power and authority to decide
theological controversies at a moment's notice, in virtue of
miraculous illumination; how, in the name of Reason,
were they ignorant of this prerogative for so many centuries; or, if they were not ignorant of it, how are they not
responsible for all the divisions and heresies which have
torn the Church to pieces when a word would have put an
end to them? That there should be such prolonged uncertainty even on *points* of Faith is hardly compatible with
your view as to Christ's promise of theological uniformity. But that the very *rule* of faith itself should need to be
defined in 1870 is manifestly incredible. You tell us that the
papal infallibility is Christ's divinely instituted means for
securing doctrinal uniformity and certitude; and yet this
doctrine was itself uncertain for nearly two thousand

years! Never was there a more vicious circle.

No, Your Eminence. The dogmas and definitions of popes and councils on their theological side are but the protective husks of revelation—of the Gospel of Christ. It is only the revealed kernel and not the theological husk to which they can bind our consciences. If they add a jot or tittle to the easy yoke and light burden of Christ's teaching, let them be anathema.

Let us face facts. The Way and the Life and the Truth have been made plain to the simplest from the very beginning. The truths by which our souls live and are sanctified are few, and are clear to all. About further points, theological uncertainty is not of the slightest direct spiritual consequence for the individual; it may often be more wholesome than certainty. And so to pretend that Christ ought to have and therefore must have provided for theological uniformity is to fly in the face of facts and to misapprehend the scope and meaning of the Gospel as summed up in the words: "Repent, for the Kingdom of Heaven is at hand." This confusion of Faith with theology, and of unity of Faith with theological uniformity, is of course one of the main supports of the individualistic interpretation of the Vatican Decrees and of the refusal to recognise the collective spirit of the whole Church as the one rule of faith.

IV

THE SUPPOSED CONSTITUTION
OF THE CHURCH

AND now I pass to your conception of the constitution of the Church as shaped by this supposed necessity of theological uniformity, as well as by a confusion of military with spiritual government and authority. Like all speculative errors, these live and thrive in virtue of the services they render to certain interests often very human and unspiritual. That one Church should claim a monopoly of correct doctrine and of all jurisdiction; that it should desire to exalt itself at the expense of all the rest and become the one centre of all spiritual and temporal dominion is natural. That it should be able to do so, implies that there must be at least some apparent justification for a claim which else the other equally human Churches would as naturally contest.

You tell us, then, that Christ gave all his powers, not to the whole Church collectively, but to the Apostles and to their successors the bishops united to the Pope. For the moment you forget that every Christian can confer the greatest of all the sacraments —baptism; not to speak of the sacrament of matrimony.

You say it is only the episcopate united with the Pope that has the right to interpret revelation officially. If you mean that it is their office to gather up, formulate, and proclaim the sacred tradition which lives in the collective conscience of the whole Church *Discens* and *Docens*, lay and cleric, it is what every true Catholic holds. If you mean

that the tradition lives exclusively in the collective episcopal conscience, or still worse (as you undoubtedly mean)
in the single conscience of the Pope, your meaning is
repudiated by all the Churches of the East and was
vehemently disputed in the West till, in 1870, it was
apparently but not really approved by the Vatican Council. If you are right, the whole Church was in error about
her essential constitution for many centuries of her existence. You speak as though the episcopate were the whole
Church commissioned to convert and evangelise the lower
clergy and the laity. You forget that the lower clergy and
laity are part of the Church which, as a whole, has been
commissioned to convert and evangelise the world; that to
the whole Church, and not merely to the Apostles, it was
said "Go and teach all nations." You forget that every
baptised Christian is a commissioned apostle and teacher;
and as such is no mere telephone, but must speak from the
fulness of a living personal interest in the truth of his
religion; that he must *think* his faith and penetrate and
develop it according to the measure of his education and
understanding. You would have us believe that the layman's sole duty is to receive the faith passively as one
receives a traveller's tale of regions beyond his ken; a tale
which he repeats to others word for word for what it is
worth, but with no guarantee of personal experience or
conviction. And then you wonder that your passively
receptive flock are not interested in their religion; that they
do not feel themselves in any way responsible for its
teaching; and you search in vain for a New Testament or
a Roman Missal in the libraries of educated Catholics !

No Catholic denies the useful distinction between the
"Church Teaching" and the "Church Taught." It is obvi-
ously necessary that at any given time Christians should
know what they all hold in common and what is peculiar
to themselves; that they should not require of others more
than the Universal Church requires; and it is for the
assembled episcopate to determine this minimum; to bear

59

witness to the accordant beliefs of their several dioceses and to impose the common faith on each particular member of the Church, be he layman, bishop, or Pope. If we bow to such rulings of the teaching Church, it is just in the measure that the moral unanimity of a truly free and representative council is presumably and at least practically equivalent to a consensus of the whole body of believers. It is only a presumption; one that may be and has often been rebutted. The ecumenicity of a council is to some degree always a fiction—though a necessary fiction in the interests of order and unity. What we really bow to is a Divine Tradition of which the entire Church, and not merely the episcopate, is the organ and depositary; to which we attribute just the same sort of inerrancy, neither more nor less, that we attribute to the Sacred Scriptures, which are after all but a few chance leaves torn from the book of tradition.

I notice that you say, "The episcopate in union with the Pope is the organ of transmission of the revealed teachings of Jesus Christ. Be it said, in passing (*en passant*), that the organ of transmission is what, in one word, is called Tradition."

This "*en passant*" is surely significant. It indicates your consciousness that there is here something out of joint; something not quite coherent with your simplification, but which cannot be ignored with any respect to the history of dogma. "The organ of transmission is the episcopate"; "The organ of transmission is Tradition"—these statements are not very harmonious. I should have thought that Tradition was the process of transmission or else the thing transmitted, and not the organ of transmission. But for this confusion you have excellent precedent in the words of Pius IX, *La tradizione son io*, framed on the analogy of "L'État c'est moi."

Tradition may be used for the process of passing on, or for that which is passed on, but not for the persons who pass it on. Even if the episcopate be the sole depositary of tradition and the sole organ of its transmission, we cannot say that the episcopate or the Pope *is* tradition. If Your Eminence will reflect a moment it will be clear that tradition is to the episcopate or to the Pope what the law is to the judge. It is a rule set above them by a higher authority; a rule which they must apply and interpret, but which they did not make and may not alter. Tradition is the faith that lives in the whole Church and is handed down from generation to generation, of which the entire body, and not a mere handful of officials, is the depositary and organ of transmission. Of this rule and law the Holy Spirit diffused in the hearts of all the faithful is the author; the episcopate merely the servant, the witness, the interpreter.

But I question whether, even on your own grounds, you have any right to say, "Tradition is the Episcopate" and not rather "Tradition is the Pope"—*La tradizione son io.*

You speak always of "The Episcopate in union with the Pope," or "The bishops who are in agreement with the Pope," as the final authority in matters of doctrine. In deference to history you cannot very well leave out the bishops; but the condition which you impose on their authority renders their existence purely ornamental and nugatory. They really interfere with your simplification; and that you should have to tolerate such a discordant element does credit at least to your uneasy historical conscience. If there is still a nominal episcopate it is not the fault of the Curialists, or their new theology. For if I can trust a certain body of witnesses only when their testimony agrees with that of one particular witness; if the testimony of this one alone is quite sufficient without theirs, is not their testimony utterly superfluous and worthless? Why should I trouble about the bishops at all, if I must first find out whether they agree with the Pope? Is it not as though a Protestant were to say that his supreme rule of faith was the episcopate so far as in agreement with the Bible? Do you not see that this is equivalent to saying that the Bible, and the Bible only, is his rule of faith? Do you not see that your own expression means that the Pope and the Pope only is the rule of Faith?—that we must sit in judgment on our bishops and test their orthodoxy by this rule?

But the new theology drags the bishops into the formula to conceal the fact that the whole constitution of the Church has been turned upside down by this new-fashioned individualistic interpretation of the papacy.

Your bishops are simply on parade at a papal ceremony. You may *call* them "co-judges" and "co-definers"; but they are not. Their judgment counts for absolutely nothing. Their sole honour is to lead the chorus of universal acclaim and passive submission as the principal representatives of the *Ecclesia Discens*. If they "teach" by transmitting what they learn from the Pope, so does every simple priest and every lay catechist. Let us not pay ourselves with words. The episcopate singly and collectively has passed over to the *Ecclesia Discens* and the Pope alone is the *Ecclesia Docens*—"La tradizione son io." If no bishop or number of bishops can hinder the Pope's dogmatic decision, in what sense can they be considered as joint-authors of that decision? As theological consultors they rank no higher than simple priests who belong to the *Ecclesia Discens*.

What difference do you make between the bishops and the *Ecclesia Discens* in relation to the Pope, when you write "Whenever a doctrinal dispute breaks out among the faithful *or among the bishops*, the Pope settles it by his supreme authority"?

Guard your words how you will, your thought leaks out between them at every turn.

It is better, then, to state this simplification honestly and nakedly, instead of hiding its shame with the rags of the ancient Catholic tradition.

The Pope *is* the Church. To him alone Christ has committed the apostolic mission, the deposit of revelation, the plenitude of doctrinal authority and of spiritual power and jurisdiction. Him alone he has commissioned to teach and sanctify, not the world, but the bishops, the clergy, and the faithful: "Feed my sheep; feed my lambs." If the episcopal or clerical sheep have any doctrinal or spiritual power over the lambs it is as mere delegates of the Pope, as streams deriving from that single fountain of all supernatural life and teaching. The shepherd is no part of his flock. He stands outside and above it as a being of another and higher species. They are absolutely passive and receptive under his guidance. They have no mind or will of their own singly or collectively.

"The doctrinal and juridical authority of the Church," writes P. Liberatore, S.J., in 1871 "is gathered up and concentrated in the Roman Pontiff. From his chair springs the light that is blazed and spread abroad to enlighten the universe. His throne is exalted above the thrones of all subordinate prelates, and from the tiara that circles his brow stream forth the rays that are reflected from the episcopal mitres of the whole world." Thus the bishops shine merely as planets with a light borrowed from the Pope—the sun and sole source of their illumination.

The individual mind and will of the Pope (miraculously illuminated, of course) is precisely the mind and will of the Church. I do not know by what courtesy the bishops are still called shepherds, except it be that those sheep who follow the shepherd are, for purposes of guidance, as good as the shepherd himself. But at that rate it seems to me that any good Catholic "in union with the Pope" might be called a shepherd and a member of the *Ecclesia Docens*. In this view it were of course absurd to regard the collective mind of the flock as the depositary and organ of that divine tradition of whose sense the Pope is the sole judge. "La tradizione son io"—it is only into the depths of his own religious conscience that the shepherd need look to discover the truth needed for the guidance of his mindless flock.

Your Eminence: a boy in his teens,* as ignorant as he was morally vicious, was once elected to be the Vicar of Christ. He had not at the moment of his election the most rudimentary knowledge of his Catechism. You maintain that the great Christian tradition and deposit of Faith was suddenly infused into that empty godless little brain; that he had only to look within himself in order to instruct the whole episcopate as to the true sense of revelation. Plainly your Church-theory is tenable only on the supposition of a continual miracle as wonderful as the conversion of water into wine, and which would give us a right to look for a uniform and superhuman wisdom in the supreme government of the Church, for which there is not a vestige of historical evidence.

It is not wonderful, then, that you apply to the Pope the title of "bishop of bishops," which even Gregory I indignantly repudiated as a *nomen blasphemiae* and as a *maxima stultitia*. For in your new theology the Pope is related to the bishops precisely as a bishop is to his priests. Their dependence on him is absolute and unqualified. He still calls them "brethren," to conceal the breach with the ancient tradition. But they have begun to address him as Father, since, as a fact, they are no longer his brethren but his sons or, rather, his servants. They are bound to obey with the blindness of slaves, and not even with the intelligent sympathy of sons. Yet, Your Eminence, Christ did not say to Peter "Confirm thy sons" or "thy servants," but "Confirm thy brethren"; still less did he say "Rule thy servants " —*Dominare in medio servorum tuorum*.

I notice that you distinguish this "bishop of bishops"

---

* The reference is to John XII (955-964), bastard son of Alberic II, prince of Rome. Alberic extracted a promise from the Roman nobles that they would elect his son Octavian as pope. At his election Octavian, who took the name John, was eighteen years old, notorious for debauchery and devoid of all religious sensibility. He was later deposed by a synod with the help of Otto I, King of Germany. He is accepted as a legitimate pope (Ed.).

from his servant bishops as being "the immediate representative of the Son of God." Twenty years ago my Jesuit
Professor of Theology did not venture to teach as more
than probable the view that the other Apostles drew their
authority not immediately from Christ, but only mediately
through Peter. It was then enough to say that union with
Peter was the condition of any valid exercise of their
immediately divine authority. Now we have developed a
little further. The eleven Apostles spring from Peter, the
episcopate springs from the Pope, as the branches from
the root of a tree. Once more the Pope is their father and
not their brother.

The right of command, the duty of obedience, have no
place among brethren. Their agreement must be a spiritual and spontaneous agreement. Even Christ did not lord
it over his Apostles. He was in their midst as a servant. He
called them not servants but friends. The now hollow-
sounding title of "Servant of the servants of God," which
the Pope dares not discard, bears witness to the ancient
tradition of the Church, and agrees ill with that of "Bishop
of bishops." The promises made to Peter were made to
every Apostle and bishop as such; and in the early centuries every bishop regarded himself as successor of Peter
and heir of those promises.

Formerly a bishop was the highest ecclesiastical official
in his own diocese. He was answerable to no other official,
but only to the universal Church of which he was the
organ or officer. But now that your new theology has
concentrated the universal Church into the person of the
Pope, we have a sort of double episcopate in each diocese—the Bishop of Rome and the local bishop, the latter
being merely the delegate or Vicar-General of the former.
Of this system there is not a trace in the first six centuries
of Church History, from which we learn that the Pope is
neither over the bishops as their master, nor under them
as their delegate, but alongside of them as first in the rank
of his brethren; that this teaching hierarchy is neither

above nor below the whole Church, of which it is an
organic part, and which, as a whole, lives, wills, and
speaks, not only through, but in union with, that organic
part.

How did such a revolution come about? When Christ
said to his disciples "As the living Father hath sent me, so
send I you," or, "He that heareth you heareth me," he was
not deciding "which of them should be the greatest." That
question he had answered when he set a little child in their
midst; or when he stooped down and washed their feet; or
when he warned them against the spirit of domination. He
was not giving juridical authority to the hierarchy of the
Church over the laity. Nay, he was not thinking of the
hierarchic Church at all. He was thinking of the
unconverted world and of the little band of believers—the
light of the world; the salt of the earth—which was to
continue his own apostolic mission in the same spirit and
by the same methods.

To each and all of them he gave authority and command
to preach the Gospel—not to coerce and excommunicate
one another. The internal division and organisation of that
missionary body into rulers and ruled; teachers and taught;
active and passive; the relegation of the Church's missionary work to a secondary place; the concentration of her
interest on the task of holding herself together, of securing
internal unity by subjecting one half of her members to the
other half—all this, Your Eminence, is what we poor
Modernists would call a development. At the beginning
there was not a teaching Church and a learning Church,
but a teaching Church and a learning world. Every Christian in virtue of his baptism was a teacher and apostle.

And to each and all of these apostles he communicates
his own authority; his own Spirit; his own mission: "Receive the Holy Spirit; as the Father hath sent me so send I
you."

But what sort of authority do we find him exercising in
his missionary work? Do we see him defining theological

points "under pain of eternal damnation"? I cannot remember an instance. I see that he draws men, but that he never drives them. I see a Shepherd who goes in front of his sheep and lures them on: "If any man will come after me, let him follow me." I see him exerting not a juridical but a spiritual authority—the authority that truth exercises over the mind; and goodness, over the conscience; and love, over the heart and affections; the authority that true Manhood exercises over men; true Personality, over persons.

And it was just this sort of spiritual authority that he communicated to his brethren, kindling their hearts with the fire which he came to spread upon earth, and with which his own heart was aflame. Filled with the same Holy Spirit, they were to be so fashioned to his image and likeness as to be indistinguishable from him in their enthusiasms, aims, and methods: "He that heareth you heareth me."

You will say that the Gospel was an enlightenment; that as he was "the Light of the World" so they were to be the light of the world. Yes, but what sort of light? "Let your light so shine before men that they may see your good works and glorify your Father who is in Heaven." It was not the light of a new theology, but that of a new revelation, a new experience, a new life, a new ideal of human personality. And of that ideal, the Apostles were to be the embodiment no less than their Master. He taught by what he was. Such, too, was to be the teaching authority of his Church: "Hereby shall men know that you are my disciples, if you love one another." Here is the genuine "note" of the true Church: "Behold, how these Christians love one another." It is, then, of this spiritual authority that he speaks when he says, "As the living Father hath sent me, so send I you"; "He that hath seen me hath seen the Father"; "He that heareth you, heareth me"; or when he prays "that they all may be one, as thou, Father, art in me and I in thee"—not a thought of setting some of his brethren as rulers over the rest to impose theological uniformity "under pain of eternal damnation." The revelation which he committed to them was that of the Father's divine life as faithfully imaged in his own life, and to be as faithfully imaged in that of his Church. It was the "truth" of a type to its archetype; the "truth" of a Way and a Life, not of a theory or a theology.

When the little missionary band was yet small; when it was filled with the enthusiasm of the Spirit of its Founder; when they "were all of one heart and one mind" and "possessed all things in common" there was little need of any more interior organisation than was required for successful co-operation in the work of the apostolate. When it grew to a vast multitude of men, good, bad, and indifferent, the spiritual influence of the Church in the world demanded a hierarchy of officials with juridical power to exclude from the community those whose presence was a source of discord or scandal. But it was for their unchristian lives, not for their theological opinions, that men were first excommunicated. The first case on record is that of the incestuous Corinthian.

But whereas we are under the jurisdiction of the State whether we will or no, we are under that of the Church only by our free choice. I am bound to obey her officers only as I obey my physician after I have freely put myself into his hands to be cured by him. He has no right to domineer over me. He can only say, "Unless you obey me you will die." The rule he has over me is imposed by myself. So too the rule which the Church has over me derives from my own conscience; from my own free act. All she can say to me is, "If you love me, keep my commandments." If I do not keep her commandments she can say, "You do not love me"; but she cannot coerce or threaten me. She can tell me I am in danger of hell, but she cannot send me there. Her duty is to try and make me love her once more; to draw me back to her, not to drive me away from her.

To apply to this juridical and hierarchic power of the later Church texts that refer only to the spiritual influence of the primitive and pre-hierarchic Church was possible and even excusable in an age devoid of the slightest historical and critical sense. Yet this misapplication has been and is still the main support of the medieval Church-theory. Surely it is time we had done with this superficial exegesis that has ceased to be excusable.

V

GROWTH OF THIS CONCEPTION

I T is not then very difficult to understand how this conception of the Pope's unlimited jurisdiction over doctrine and discipline was gradually evolved out of certain elementary misapprehensions.

The first pre-eminence of the Church of Rome was one of charity and good works. As S. Irenaeus tells us in a passage which you treat with a strange disregard of more recent criticism, and as though it were undisputed "Such is the superiority of the pre-eminence of the Church of Rome that the faithful from all parts of the world must necessarily meet together there." If you prefer to translate "must necessarily agree with her" it will not alter the evident meaning. In that great central ganglion of the Roman Empire one met representatives from every Christian community, and could therefore study the unanimous beliefs and practices of the whole Church.

It was the advantage of the Roman Community to be thus in continual touch with all the rest; not to dictate to them, but to learn from them what was everywhere held and believed. Hence the opinion of the Roman Church was practically that of the Church at large. Her Christianity was the typical Christianity. To be in agreement with her was to be in agreement with all. This is very different from saying that the faith of Rome was the supreme and independent criterion of faith. It was so only in so far as it reflected the unanimous faith of all the Christian communities.

70

Rome was then the most expeditious, but not the highest, court of appeal. As yet, she claimed no jurisdiction over her sister Churches. They venerated, admired, and followed her of their own free will and accord. She drew them, but she did not drive them. Peter confirmed and supported, but he did not yet rule his brethren or call them his sons or his servants. His supremacy was spiritual, not juridical. It was a duty rather than a right—a debt of edification and support and leadership which weighed more heavily upon him than upon them; an ideal which he could never realise perfectly, and from which he has fallen away utterly over and over again in the history of the Church.

Seeing herself so universally appealed to; her approval accepted as a tessera of orthodoxy; her excommunications adopted by other Churches, it was only too natural that Rome should come insensibly to regard this deference as a right, and to use the concession or withdrawal of her favour as a coercive sanction whereby to enforce her own will on her sister-Churches. Every day, in every department of society, we can witness the process by which the chosen leader among equals becomes the ruler and driver and by which his free admirers and followers become his subjects and servants.

That is the process by which the first of bishops became the "Bishop of bishops"; and by which his "venerable brethren" became his sons, his servants, and (one must now add) his marionettes. Thus it was that Rome's duty of spiritual supremacy was transformed into a right of juridical supremacy. And when the Gospel texts which refer to the former were applied to the latter, it was only a matter of time and of scholastic logic to deduce this monstrous concentration of the whole Church into the person of a single bishop. And to this development, besides motives of ecclesiastical expediency, avarice, ambition, and other passions have most undeniably lent their driving-force for centuries. The debased theology of the movement, with its

71

blind logicality, its perversion of Scripture, its distortion of the Fathers, is but the after-justification, not the real cause of the phenomenon. And though perhaps never yet has such an ideal of absolutism and irresponsibility been conceived by the mind of man, yet I doubt if this new theology be not pregnant with still further developments. We were warned at the time of the Bull about Anglican Orders that, though not *ex cathedra*, it might be infallible. For, it was said, the Vatican Decree, though inclusive only of *ex cathedra* utterances, did not exclude others. Thus Your Eminence speaks of Modernism as condemned "by the supreme authority of the Church," i.e. you ascribe the same weight to the Encyclical *Pascendi* as to the Nicene Creed. And certainly the *a priori* arguments (from "what ought to be" to "what is") as well as the fantastic exegesis which supports so much, will support a great deal more and extend infallibility quite logically to every brief and encyclical. They tell even more strongly for impeccability than for infallibility.

For does not the Pope inherit all those prerogatives of Peter that were needful for the edification of the Church? Do not theologians tell us that Peter and his fellow Apostles were "confirmed in grace" and immune from moral corruption? Can we say that the Church stands in less need of such edification today than in the apostolic age? Indeed, it would be curious if the only Petrine prerogatives not claimed by the Pope were just those which, being verifiable, would be most convincing—moral integrity and miraculous powers. If the latter was a need peculiar to the nascent Church we can hardly say the same of the former. There is, therefore, some logic in the growing tendency to treat the Pope as impeccable and above criticism in matters of discipline and government; to render him the personal cultus hitherto reserved for canonised saints.

Again, if you interpret "Whatsoever thou shalt bind on earth shall be bound in heaven" as conferring juridical not spiritual authority, must you not go further and confess that God is the Pope's Vicar in heaven, the passively obedient executor of his will? One of your candid brethren, the Cardinal Archbishop of Salzburg, in his Pastoral of February 2nd, 1905, does not hesitate to say openly what you all think when he writes: "O inconceivably exalted power! heaven suffers earth to prescribe the kind and measure of its decisions; the servant is made the judge of the world and his Master in heaven ratifies the sentence which he pronounces on earth." Thus God Himself is brought down to the level of a bishop and takes his orders from Rome; and in giving the Keys of the Kingdom to Peter Christ has become a *roi fainéant*.

Your Eminence, on the communion-tessera of this year, approved by the Archbishop of Milan, I find Mary and the Pope twice put side by side: *Gloria alla Madre Immacolatta: Gloria al santo Padre!* I have seen one of the crosses sold to the faithful of Rome on which the figure of Christ is replaced by that of the Pope. I admit the logic of it all, but I ask myself: Where is it to end? Have we yet to learn the immaculate conception of the Pope, or his real presence in the Sacrament of the Altar? May I not justly ask: "Was Pius crucified for you, or were you baptised in the name of Pius"? (cf. 1 Cor. 1:13). Can you wonder if Protestants speak of "Papolatry" or of the Pope as the anti-Christ who sets himself up as God in the temple of God?*

Such a system could never have obtained a moment's credence; could never have survived for so many centuries, had it not presented to good and spiritual men a certain deceptive plausibility. Over and above the theological sophistries advanced in its support there were various practical reasons of religious expediency which weighed with those who would never have listened to reasons of merely political and temporal expediency. Unity, they believed rightly, was the "note" of the true

---

* See Note on p. 170.

Church. But understanding unity as military and mechanical uniformity, rather than as the free agreement of independent spirits in faith, aim, and sentiment, they inferred, again rightly, that such uniformity could only be secured by a military dictatorship; that Christ must have made provision for so vital a necessity, and that, in spite of all contrary evidence, Scripture and Church History must be interpreted so as to confirm, or, at least, not to exclude, this hypothesis.

But granted for the moment that unity of theological formula was to be the note of the true Church and the abiding miracle in evidence of her claims, would not that evidence have been far more striking had the whole multitude of the faithful been moved spontaneously and independently to such an agreement; or even had the bishops, without the somewhat natural expedient of councils, disputations, wranglings, and intrigues, been found ever saying just the same thing? It would have meant a miracle. But this uniformity is supposed to be miraculous. I have already noted that the knowledge and infallible interpretation of tradition by a totally ignorant boy-Pope like John XII or Benedict IX would be an effect without a natural cause; and in some great measure this must be true of every Pope. Now whereas the independent theological unity of the episcopate would be a verifiable and serviceable miracle, the uniformity secured by their blind submission to the Pope is as natural as that of a regiment of soldiers. It is only the testimony of independent witnesses that has the slightest evidential significance. If, then, we are to reason *a priori* as to what God ought to, and therefore must, have done, it is quite plain that he ought to have provided for the verifiable miracle of spontaneous episcopal unity, rather than for a perfectly explicable unity secured by obedience to a dictator, the miracle of whose infallibility can never be verified.

That God has made no such provision, may mean that theology is not yet quite in a position to determine exactly what he ought to do; or it may even mean that he does not attach quite as much importance to theological uniformity as theologians suppose.

Similarly as regards the concentration of all the Church's juridical authority into the person of the Pope alone. It is defensible as the natural and necessary means of securing military uniformity of action, without which the Church must cease to be a great international power, fighting political battles with political weapons. But who gave the Church any such mission? And where is there any trace of such pretensions in the first centuries of her existence? Her mission was to announce the coming Kingdom of God upon earth—an event whose accomplishment lay in his hands and not in hers—and to preach repentance and a new life to individual souls as the necessary condition of entering into that Kingdom. Every man whatever his profession or occupation, be he politician, soldier, physician, savant, artist, merchant or what you will, who labours for the general good, and for the cause of justice and truth, is labouring for the Kingdom of God on earth. The Church's concern is not directly with these things. She has no infallible *charisma* in political, legal, scientific, and economic problems. Her work is the formation of individual souls to the pattern of Christ; the production of character, the elevation of ideals. Her mission is to impress upon every man the duty of living, not for himself, but for the common good, for the Kingdom of God, according to the opportunities of his station; to kindle in each that fire of self-devotion which Christ came to kindle upon earth; to stimulate faith, hope, and enthusiasm in the cause of an Ideal before whose immensity and remoteness the unaided spirit grows weary and discouraged. For without such faith and hope who could struggle for the reign of truth and justice upon earth? What were it all worth if after a few hundred thousand years human history will matter as little as that of any other extinct species; and if it have not in some way the eternal value of an episode in the life of the Eternal? It is religion alone that can give an infinite and absolute value to humanity and to the service of humanity.

Does such a mission demand a centralised military organisation? Is the immense and complicated bureaucracy of Rome solely preoccupied with the sanctification of individual souls; with repentance and a new life; with the mission of John the Baptist and of Jesus? No serious man will say so. It is only the idea that the Church's mission is to control the business of the whole world instead of teaching every man to regard his own business as the work of God, that can account for this extraordinary "development" of the Gospel. When every man is a good Christian things will set themselves right quickly enough; the Kingdom of God will come without observation; will be found in our midst while we are looking for it in the clouds. That is an infinitely distant goal or ideal. But it is one to which we must ever approximate; and each new stage is, relatively to the preceding, a realisation of the Kingdom of God.

"In necessariis unitas; in dubiis libertas; in omnibus caritas"—unity in essentials, liberty in non-essentials; charity in all things. But I ask myself, Are not the essentials far fewer than your new theology supposes? " One Lord," Jesus Christ; "One faith" in the coming Kingdom of God; "one baptism" to repentance and a new life. May not this be the "one thing needful"? May not all the rest be permissible, most desirable, but not obligatory? May not the mutual charity that tolerates differences in non-essentials be a higher unity than that of enforced uniformity?

Who can read the Gospel and not feel that its clear quiet light is dimmed and broken with all this wire-netting of intricate theology by which we pretend to protect it from profanation? Since we own that theology can add nothing to it that binds our faith, that dogmas but render its implications explicit, why not be content with the simple, inspired, unelaborated expression of revelation? Is it not enough to believe what Peter believed? One thing is certain. If instead of wrangling over disputed questions about which we can know nothing, and of which it would not profit us to know everything, ecumenical councils had preached liberty in non-essentials; had rebuked the contentious spirit of theology; had recalled men to the simple revelation of the Gospel; had proclaimed crusades against slavery, dishonesty, intemperance, cruelty, oppression; had striven to purify and develop the Christian ideal of character, the face of the world to-day would be very different from what it is. Or, again—and here, for once, Pius X will uphold me—if men had always been able to look to the Bishop and Church of Rome for a living example of authentic Christianity, individual and social; if the Vatican had been always officered with apostolic men, like the early Christians or the early Franciscans, preoccupied entirely with the salvation of souls, and not with an intriguing, worldly, often loose-living bureaucracy for whom centralisation meant money and influence, Rome might still possess that supreme spiritual authority which for centuries has been in abeyance—she might still be the salt of the earth and the light of the world; the abiding revelation of that new life made known to us in and by Christ.

How unreal all this seems compared with what she has been historically! How often has not he, whose duty was "to confirm his brethren," to draw them together by the force of good example, been the author of irreparable scandals and divisions? Is it not the Popes who with the sword of theological omniscience in one hand and that of juridical omnipotence in the other have hacked the whole body of Christendom to pieces; have split the East from the West, the Teutonic from the Latin races; the whole Church from the living world? And all this under the pretext of securing a sterilising insignificant external uniformity —spiritually worthless and even disastrous; a uniformity that sucks the life out of the whole body of the Church for the benefit of the head, that substitutes the judgment, will, and action of a single individual for that of the *orbis terrarum*.

"Eh bien," you say, "eh bien, mes Frères, le Modernisme que le Pape a condamné est la négation de ces enseignements si simples que vous avez appris dès votre enfance lorsque vous vous prépariez à la première communion."

Yes, Your Eminence, a doctrine "so simple" that it quietly leaves out of account the host of unanswerable difficulties—scriptural, historical, and rational—that have been raised against it; "so simple" as to be absolutely uninteresting and devitalising; "so simple" that having once mastered it at their first communion the faithful feel no reason ever to give it another thought. To obey the Pope and to ask no questions—that is the whole of religion, not only for laymen, but for priests and bishops.

VI

THE VATICAN DEFINITION

AND now if I have taken some trouble to expose this great medieval simplification; to strip it bare of the garment of antiquity under which its novelty is disguised—of certain terms and forms of Catholicism under which it has slipped another and contrary meaning—it is because I acknowledge freely that in this view of the Papacy your Eminence is at one with the Pope and the whole Roman officialdom; with nearly all the bishops; with the greater part of the lower clergy and with a still greater proportion of the laity. Still I do not think that a numerical majority is the same thing as that moral unanimity which constitutes the *consensus ecclesiae*. Moreover I do not for a moment believe that the agreement of the said majority is that of free and independent witnesses, or that it represents the independent judgment of more than a very small handful of interested theologians and officials.

"But," you will say, "it is that of the Vatican Council; and there is an end of the matter."

That is what I beg to deny, since my whole position as a Roman Catholic depends on my denying it; on my being able, if necessary by some *tour de force*, to show that the Vatican Council did not succeed in its efforts to turn the Church upside down and to rest the hierarchical pyramid on its apex.

I know this requires a certain amount of ingenuity, a

certain risk of sophistry; but not more than that of Tract XC by which Cardinal Newman read the doctrine of Trent into the Thirty-nine Articles of the Church of England.

All that the Fathers of the Church have said as to the inerrancy of General Councils and of sacred tradition is as nothing to what they have said as to the inerrancy of those classical pages of tradition which we call the Bible. With all due deference to the Biblical Commission and the Holy Office, the hard and fast mechanical view of Scriptural inerrancy has yielded for ever to a much looser, more flexible and dynamic notion of inspiration. The old conception is as dead as the Ptolemaic astronomy; those who cling to it will die with it. The inerrancy of General Councils must inevitably and *a fortiori* be re-interpreted with a similar latitude.

For this reason Catholics are justified in interpreting the utterances of authority with a considerably greater latitude than formerly.

Again, I think it might be very plausibly argued by any one who has studied the history of the Vatican Council that it lacked every one of the three conditions of a valid council—that it was neither free, nor representative nor unanimous; that the bishops were bullied and coerced; were kept in ignorance of the programme till the last moment; were deprived of the necessary sources of information; were forbidden liberty of discussion among themselves; that the Council was packed with bishops *in partibus* representing nobody; with Italian bishops representing next to nobody; while vast populations outside Italy were hardly represented at all; that, by an unconscious assimilation of the Church's constitution to that of a modern popular government, the voice of a bare numerical majority was substituted for the morally unanimous voice of the whole assembly; and finally that the appearance of unanimity secured by the cowardly withdrawal of the dissentient minority was purely illusory.

Such was the contention of the great and staunchly

Catholic Dr. Döllinger and of many other equally competent judges. But it is one that does not commend itself to
me, because I know that some of the most important
councils that the Church has accepted could be easily
invalidated by a similar criticism. Again, I think it may be
plausibly urged by the Old Catholics that the subsequent
acquiescence of the Roman Church in the Vatican decree
does not constitute an *argumentun ad hominem* against
them and others who make the Christian *orbis terrarum* the
supreme judge of faith which the Council represents more
or less imperfectly.

For, first of all, they may say that the dissent of the
whole Eastern Church and episcopate is a somewhat
serious difficulty. Then, it is easy to show that this passive
acquiescence is a very different thing from a free, independent acceptance; that an imposed listless uniformity
lacks all the evidential value of a spontaneous active
unanimity. We know how those who for generations
previously had been working for the definition of Papal
absolutism, who engineered the Vatican Council purely in
that interest, who all but succeeded in committing the
Roman Church to that novelty, at once set out to remedy
the little flaws in their handiwork; to obscure and cover up
the loopholes which the definition left unwillingly in its
attempt to wall-up the fundamental principles of Catholicism—*Securus judicat orbis terrarum* and *Quod semper, quod
ubique quod ab omnibus*. To ignore the possibility of a
Catholic interpretation; to speak as though they had
succeeded in their design; to brand and defame as heretics
those who thought otherwise; to reform the catechisms
and seminary manuals in their own sense; to select as
professors and bishops only obsequious zealots in the
cause of absolutism—all this, and much more was only a
matter of governmental ingenuity. After two generations
could the results be other than what they are? Who can see
the work of the Holy Ghost in the agreement of bishops
selected because they agree to be bishops no longer but

delegates of the one and only bishop; or in that of priests still more utterly depersonalised; or in that of a listless and indifferent laity—schooled, till their first communion, in this easy thought-saving simplification, and subsequently dead to all further interest in the matter?

Yet I do not urge this objection, for, again, I feel it is one that would tell equally against many a more venerable council. I ask myself whether a consensus in purely theological matters could ever possibly be more than that of a mere handful of experts; whether the general acquiescence of the crowd can have the slightest confirmatory value, any more than that of a class of schoolboys can be said to confirm the teachings of their master. It is only the perfectly spontaneous agreement of spirit with spirit that lends value to a consensus. If it is the result of listlessness, or of imitativeness, or of governmental pressure, or of the fear of eternal damnation, it is worthless.

A general consensus of the faithful can only obtain in regard to those matters where all may be experts; matters within the potential experience of each; matters which interest and affect their daily spiritual life—the life of faith in virtue of which they are called "the faithful." If I want to be sure of the normality of my own senses; to know that my perceptions are objective and not subjective, I take the judgment of the crowd as my criterion. If, however, it is a question, not of ordinary and universal experience, but of learning, information, and reflection; not of phenomena, but of the analysis and interpretation of phenomena, it would be absurd to appeal to the crowd. If Faith were theology its problems could never be settled by general consensus.

But because it is not theology, but the Gospel; because its object is that life of which Christ is the Divine Revelation, and not the analysis of that life, every believer may, as an expert, speak of his own personal response to the Gospel. Each is a judge of faith; and the agreement of all is an infallible judgment, eliminating private errors and idiosyncrasies.

The metaphysical decisions arrived at by many of the great councils were certainly not such as could receive the slightest confirmation from the subsequent general consent of the Church. What could ordinary Christian experience witness as to the precise mode of the Eucharistic presence, or as to the curious problems about grace? Indeed, it is difficult to imagine how there could be any sort of significant acceptance of propositions that, when closely examined, are often found to be mere collocations of words, to which even theologians, if pressed, are unable to attach the slightest intelligible meaning.

But ask the faithful about the substance of Revelation, about the coming Kingdom of God on earth, about their ideals of the new life, social and individual, and at once you touch a vital interest. They will answer you from their own personal experience as independent witnesses. In fine, their consensus is a criterion of faith, but not of theology. Their subsequent acquiescence in the Vatican Decrees cannot, therefore, have the slightest confirmatory value. Its causes are purely extrinsic; but in no way connected with their religious experience or judgment.

As far as this objection goes, I cannot therefore see that the Vatican Council is in a much worse case than other councils. It is not the explicit theology of such councils, but their implicit reassertion of the Christian revelation that has represented and has been confirmed by the faith of the whole Church. Such a distinction is precisely equivalent to that which we have been forced to acknowledge between the scientific, historic, and philosophic values and the religious value of the Sacred Scriptures.

But apart from this distinction, there are other reasons for believing that the Fathers of the Vatican Council did not really succeed in cutting the Roman Church off from the ancient Catholic tradition. If Bishop Strossmayer, the ablest and most vigorous opponent of the majority, subscribed to the decrees in the end, it was because he felt and said that, as far as the purposes of the absolutists were concerned, they were not worth the paper they were written on.

It is not necessary to ascribe this failure of the absolutists to the miraculous intervention of Providence saving the Church at this suicidal moment. There are things that men cannot do even if they would. They cannot make contradictories true at the same moment, or deny a principle in virtue of itself. They cannot in the very exercise of authority cut away the root of that authority. Such was the impossible task which the absolutists set before themselves; and the result is naturally a tangle of contradictions.

When we find a document asserting or implying certain universal and fundamental principles, and at the same time making statements apparently or really in contradiction with the same, it is plain that our choice must be in favour of the more universal and fundamental principles; that ambiguous statements must be interpreted in agreement with them; that contradictory statements must be quietly ignored.

Now, though it was the deepest desire of the absolutist majority to merge the episcopate into the papacy, to eliminate every vestige of power that might in any way act as a check on Rome's claim to the monopoly of ecclesiastical power, to juridical omnipotence and theological omniscience, yet for very shame they dared not define boldly what they desired. They were forced to speak of the bishops as of co-judges and co-definers; to give them an infallibility when "in union with the Pope." As I have shown before (p. 61), this qualification of the utter nonentity of the episcopate is meaningless and merely verbal. Still, it acknowledges tacitly that the Council has no power to abolish the episcopate; that, so far as it seems to do so, it may be ignored.

Again, it is a fundamental principle that Councils may not introduce new doctrines. Their function is to check

84

innovation; to affirm that which was from the beginning. Therefore the Vatican Council cannot validly claim more for the Pope than the Popes of the early centuries claimed for themselves; it cannot make the Pope "bishop of bishops" in the sense of our new popular catechisms and theology-manuals; in the sense repudiated as foolish and blasphemous by Gregory the Great.

Again, while a Council may claim to define points of faith according to the rule of faith, it cannot define the rule of faith itself; it cannot define what is presupposed to all its definitions. So far, then, as the Vatican Council seems to suppose that the very rule of faith itself (on whose childlike simplicity and self-evidence your Eminence insists) was unknown or disputed till it was defined in 1870, it is in patent contradiction with first principles.

Again, the Council tells us that the infallibility of the Pope is not other than that which belongs to the whole Church.

This may mean either that the Church is said to be infallible only because she possesses an infallible Pope— much as a flock of sheep in union with its shepherd might be called intelligent. Or it may mean that the Pope—like the Council—speaks *ex cathedra* and infallibly only when and so far as he truly represents and utters the general mind of the Church—when he gives a judgment that is infallible, just because he speaks in union with the whole Church—not as over it or under it, but as organically one with it. The former meaning is that of the party which convoked and engineered the Council; the latter is that which they desired to but dared not openly exclude.

Lastly, when we are told that the Pope's power is "ordinary" in every diocese, it may mean that in each diocese there are two bishops with a right to ordain, confirm, govern, instruct; of whom one, the local bishop, acts merely as the vicar of the universal "bishop of bishops." And this is what the absolutists wanted to but dared not quite say. Or it may mean that although the bishop is the highest ecclesiastical official in his own diocese (of which he is the sole and not the joint spouse), yet he is responsible to the universal church, whose officer he is, and in whose name some other bishop (as a fact, the bishop of Rome) may be commissioned to speak and act. The immanence of an organism in all its parts does not mean a doubting of those parts. The local and the universal Church are not two churches.

By such criticisms it is not hard to show, with Bishop Strossmayer, that so far as the intentions of the absolutists are concerned, the Vatican Decrees are not worth the paper they are written on; that they have failed to commit the Church of Rome to heresy; that it is possible for a moderately honest man to subscribe to them without denying his Catholicism.

For this reason, while holding to the absolute soundness of Dr. Döllinger's Catholicism and sympathising with his impatience of dialectical subtleties, I venture to think that Cardinal Newman's and Bishop Strossmayer's attitude towards the Vatican Decrees was the wiser one.

VII

" THE APOSTATE DÖLLINGER "

AND since Your Eminence has thought well to drag the venerated name of Ignaz von Döllinger into your pastoral polemic against Modernism; to speak of him as "the apostate Döllinger"; to find in him an embodiment of the same Protestant spirit which you have so curiously discerned in Modernism, permit me to make a remark or two about this victim of an intolerant ecclesiastical faction—the greatest, the most learned, the most loyal Roman Catholic of the last century; one who elected to suffer the extremest injury that human malice could inflict, rather than deny the fundamental principle that divides the Catholic from the Protestant conception of the Church.

It is (as I have said) the endeavour of the new theological school to persuade men that there are but two possible religious positions—the independence of every individual, or the absolute subjection of all to a single individual. The latter it calls Catholicism; all who reject it are Protestants. Since the Greek Churches and the English Church and the Roman Catholic Modernists reject it, they are all Protestants; and therefore Dr. Döllinger was a Protestant. A serviceable and simple theology for first communicants; but surely a little immature! No doubt it is expedient in the interests of absolutism to hold up such defenders of Catholic liberty to the execration of the credulous multitude, to brand them exultantly as heretics and apostates.

The listless crowd loves ready-made judgments, and will not inquire too closely into their value. Döllinger the Protestant and Apostate; Tyrrell the far-off echo of Döllinger—that is so simple, so easy to remember.

The process by which a government buries its iniquities in oblivion and stamps the memory of its victims with infamy is more ingenious than creditable. When Dr. Döllinger defended himself so conclusively against the charge of heresy and apostasy, which of his calumniators attempted to face his reasons? They knew they had only to assert and reassert; and that in course of time, when the man was dead and the controversy forgotten, the docile, indifferent multitude would go on speaking of "Döllinger the Apostate" to the end of time. But, Your Eminence, there is no prescription for crime; and injustice is not cured by mere lapse of years. Not only in the judgment of God, but in that of sober history the name of Döllinger will be honoured and revered when those of his insignificant tormentors shall have passed out of memory—"In memoria aeterna erit justus, ab auditione mala non timebit." An apostate means, both by usage and etymology, one who stands away or separates himself from the position he formerly occupied. Dr. Döllinger could say with absolute truthfulness that, to the end of his days, he maintained the same idea of the Church's constitution which he had believed all his life, and which he had taught openly with full ecclesiastical approval for about thirty years prior to 1870.

You will say: Since he always taught the infallibility of ecumenical councils, he apostatised from that position in refusing the Vatican Decrees.

But a valid and truly ecumenical council must be unquestionably representative; perfectly free and spontaneous; morally unanimous in its decisions. Understanding the Vatican Decrees as they are most generally understood; not distinguishing, with Strossmayer, between what the majority wanted to define and what they actually succeeded in defining; conceiving that the decrees turned the constitution of the Church upside down,* rested the whole fabric on the shoulders of a single individual, abolished the distinctive principle of Catholicism, flung a contemptuous defiance in the face of history and tradition, what wonder if his unshaken faith in the indefectibility of the Church drove him back on the only other exit from his perplexity—on the supposition that a council so notoriously wanting in the three conditions of validity might be ignored consistently with Catholic principles. Even if you think he erred in his estimate of the facts about the Council, your own theology will not let you deny that *ex hypothesi* he was perfectly justified in his resistance; and for this reason, to speak (and with a certain relish) of such a man as an "apostate" is monstrous. The apostasy was theirs who broke with the past and tried to commit the whole Church to their error; it was not his who stood firm as a rock in his old position and let the angry waters rush by.

Your Eminence, I do not know any theologian, however ultramontane, who as yet teaches that the Pope is infallible when he excommunicates, or that there never can be, or never have been, excommuncations unjust and invalid owing to the ignorance or wickedness of the ecclesiastical judges. The fact that a man is excommunicate does not justify us in speaking of him as an apostate in default of other evidence. The excommunicate is one who is thrown

---

*Dr. Fredrick Nielsen, in his *History of the Papacy in the Nineteenth Century*, tells us how Mgr Pie delighted the Italian and Spanish Fathers of the Vatican Council by proving the Papal infallibility from the fact that S. Peter was crucified upside down: "Thus the Pope, as the head, now bears the whole Church; but it is he who bears and not that which is borne, that is infallible." And it is by such trivialities, by such puns and metaphors and fanciful conceits that the new theology hopes to batter down the concordant and irrefragable testimony of history! Is it not a dangerous admission that the Vicar of Christ has turned Christianity upside down?

89

overboard into the sea. The apostate is one who, by an act of suicide, leaps overboard. No doubt they are both in the water, and how they got there seems to matter little. But truth matters a good deal, and even an excommunicate is protected by the commandment which says: "Thou shalt not bear false witness against thy neighbour."

When you speak of Dr. Döllinger as an embodiment of the Protestant spirit; as infected by the Protestant atmosphere of a German University; as influencccl by the revolutionary principles of J. J. Rousseau, you force me to wonder whether your manifold preoccupations, practical and philosophical, have permitted you to read a single line of the author whom you can so stigmatise. The most superficial acquaintance with his works shows him as a deeply, even obstinately, conservative thinker, building his conclusions solely on the basis of that historical science of which he was one of the greatest masters. If, in your eyes, he erred, it was by his too rigid fidelity to antiquity, his refusal to move on with the innovators. Döllinger a Protestant! Döllinger a disciple of Rousseau! A dog is more like to a fish than he to your presentment of him. The only way I can explain such an extraordinary aberration of judgment is that, as I have said, every one is a Protestant, for Your Eminence, who is not an ultramontane; that for you there is no middle position between the absolute religious independence of each individual and the absolulte subjection of all to a single individual. At that rate the whole Church has been Protestant for centuries and only discovered her mistake for certain in 1870.

No doubt the atmosphere of German universities counted for something in the formation of Dr. Döllinger's mind. No doubt it is partly responsible for the Protestant spirit, the latent Modernism, you deplore in so many of the German clergy of today in whom the disease has not yet declared itself openly. But I should have thought that the characteristic of German universities was not so much their Protestantism as their sober regard for facts and realities; their respect for the rights of history and science; their spirit of patient and laborious investigation. The dangers you deplore belong to universities as such, and not as German. In the measure that a university is free from them it is not a university at all, but a seminary parading as a university.

If you can find Protestantism in Döllinger, it is not wonderful that you find it in Modernism. Döllinger was even less of a Modernist than Newman. What they both had in common with Modernism was the Catholic and traditional conception of the Church's constitution; the supremacy of the *orbis terrarum*, of the totality of the Church, over even the highest of her representatives and interpreters; over bishops, councils, and Popes. If Newman, like Strossmayer, accepted the Vatican Decrees, it was because he could interpret them in a Catholic sense, as once he had interpreted the Thirty-nine Articles of the Church of England. Döllinger found it easier and less equivocal to go to the root of the matter and deny the validity of the Council. Again, Döllinger's acknowledgment of the irrepressible rights of history is shared by every true Modernist. But his historical studies did not bring him face to face with those same facts concerning biblical and ecclesiastical origins which constitute the special problem for Modernism. He cannot properly be called a Modernist who does not belong to the present generation or feel the burden of its peculiar perplexities and doubts.

Yet when Your Eminence comes to describe the soul and essence of Modernism, one looks in vain for any note to distinguish it from the position of Döllinger. It apparently consists simply and only in Döllinger's contention that "The bishops sit in Council as witnesses to the faith of their flock; and that the resulting definitions should express the beliefs of the entire collectivity." It consists, you say, in this "fundamental error of Döllinger, i.e. in the parent-idea of Protestantism." Was there ever such a paradox? The principle of Tradition, the essential idea of Catholicism, put forward as the essential idea of Protestantism! When you add that thus "The agreement of individual minds is substituted for the direction of authority," can you not see that to make the *agreement* of individual minds a rule of belief is at once to set up an authority over the separate individual minds; that it is to deny flatly your contention that Modernism "rejects the doctrinal authority of the Church"? Is it not plain, as I have insisted, that you can conceive no alternative between the individualism of anarchy and that of a dictatorship; that the Catholic and social conception of authority has simply vanished from the ultramontane consciousness? In no other way is it possible to account for the hopeless confusion of your argument. When you put forward my own view, more or less in my own words, you show by your italics, already referred to (p. 47), that the consentient life and thought of the Church have no more authority in your eyes than the life and thought of a private individual; that it is a summation of zeros. You argue as though twenty men could not lift a weight together because none of them could lift it singly. You forget that the oneness which Christ desired for his Church and which was to be the note of her truth and authority, was an "agreement of individual minds"—"That they all may be one . . . so that the world may believe that thou hast sent me."

VIII

THE SUPPOSED ESSENCE
OF PROTESTANTISM

AND now when I turn to examine this "Spirit of Protestantism" which you discover in its direct antithesis, the principle of Tradition, I cannot see that your description of it is at all coherent. For, as it manifests itself in Modernism "it consists," you say, "essentially in affirming that the religious soul should draw the object and motive of its faith from itself and from itself alone": in the "rejection of any revealed communication from without." But on Your Eminence's own showing this is as false of Protestantism as it is of Modernism. For you tell us presently that Protestants draw their faith from the Bible, which they certainly regard as a "revealed communication from without" and as the word of God.

They differ, therefore, from Catholics only in that they select certain classical pages from the book of Tradition and reject a great deal of the rest. In both cases it is by an act of personal independent judgment (aided, no doubt, by grace) that the external rule of faith is accepted and its utterances then interpreted. It is by such a personal judgment that the Catholic accepts the authority of his priests, and the Protestant the authority of his Bible. It is by such a personal judgment that the Catholic interprets what his priest tells him, and the Protestant what his Bible tells him. From such a measure of "private judgment" there is no more escape for the Catholic than for the Bible Protestant. It in no way implies that impossible individualism, that religious solipsism, which you ascribe to Modernism. Such an individualism has no doubt been professed by certain quietists, Catholic as well as Protestant. But it has never been practised, for the simple reason that apart from society and social tradition a man can no more make a religion of his own than he can make a language of his own. The only question is, whether our religious mind is to be formed by society at large, or by special societies or churches set apart for the promotion of that particular social interest. With insignificant exceptions, Protestantism has always acted on the latter supposition; it has formed organised communities, with common professions and observances, for the purpose of preaching the Christian tradition as contained in the Sacred Scriptures, and of administering the rites of Baptism and Holy Communion.

When you tell us that "A Protestant Church is necessarily invisible," I ask you: "Is the Church of England (which for you is purely Protestant) invisible? Is the Lutheran Church, the Presbyterian Church, the Methodist Church invisible?" If you speak of the outward body, they are as visible as the Church of Rome; if you speak of the inward unity symbolised by the outward body, the Roman Church is as invisible as they are. God alone knows who are true Catholics in conviction and heart. Perhaps not half of those within the visible body; perhaps millions of those outside: "*Multi intus sunt qui foris videntur,*" says Augustine, and the converse is not less true—Many are outside who seem to be inside.

The pure subjectivism which you imagine to be the characteristic of Modernism and to derive from Protestantism is repudiated by both alike. A certain objective rule of faith, a certain personal acceptance and interpretation of the rule, are common to Protestantism, Catholicism, and Ultramontanism.

They differ only as to the objective rule, which is the Bible, for Protestants; the Church, including the Pope, for

Catholics; the Pope, excluding the Church, for Ultramontanes. The personal judgment by which the rule of faith is accepted and interpreted is not a private or subjective judgment. Principles, the primary dictates of Conscience and Reason, are not private opinions, but the most universal and objective of all judgments. The true distinction between Protestantism and Catholicism is that, for the former, personal interpretation is applied to the Scriptures; for the latter it is applied to Tradition. In trying, therefore, to identify Protestantism and Modernism Your Eminence betrays a complete misunderstanding of both one and the other.

It is to my Protestant education that Your Eminence traces my Modernism. You say that my kinship with Döllinger's Protestantism is "in no wise surprising, for Tyrrell is a convert whose early education was Protestant." I submit that nothing could be more surprising than that an education in a certain direction should lead to a development in the diametrically opposite direction. Either you know nothing of my antecedents or you pay a prodigious compliment to the vigour of Protestant principles. Perhaps you have read of me in certain Roman papers as an "antico pastore protestante," as one long devoted to the cause of militant anti-popery; then suddenly struck down by the blinding light of ultramontane theology; and now finally returning again like the washed sow to her wallowing in the mire. Nothing could be further from historical truth. Till the age of fifteen, I took as little interest in religious questions as any other healthy-minded schoolboy. It was from a very crude study of Bishop Butler's *Analogy* that I woke to a dim sense of there being a great and pressing world-problem to be solved for myself and for others, either positively or negatively. The same reasons that made me hope for the positive solution made me also hope that the most widespread and ancient form of Christianity might after all be found in possession of that solution. Having no adequate idea of the essential principles and differences of Potestantism and Catholicism, my objections to the latter being of a merely popular and superficial kind, it is not wonderful that at the mature age of eighteen I was ready for the step that cost a scholar like Newman half a lifetime of consideration. Not one of the reasons on which I acted do I now acknowledge as of the slightest validity. They were those of the ordinary anti-Protestant apologetic of our proselytisers—tricks of exegesis and dialectical legerdemain. The present foundations of my Catholicism are far other. At nineteen I was a Jesuit, and from that time forward my one preoccupation has been to justify the Catholic religion for myself and for others. It was in pursuit of this end that I gradually got beneath the surface and learnt, at one and the same time, the true natures and differences of Catholicism and Protestantism. As you say in your schools, "the science of contraries is one and the same science." And what I gradually learnt was, that my first apprehension of Catholicism as concentrated into the person of the Pope was theological heresy and historical ignorance; that the true and distinctive principle dividing Catholicism from Protestantism was that which barely escaped condemnation at the Vatican Council, and for adhesion to which Dr. Döllinger was excommunicated by Pius IX. And it is to my Protestant antecedents—to my six or seven years of purely passive unreasoning Protestantism—that you trace the conviction that now makes me a Catholic and prevents that return to the Church of my baptism which in so many ways would be such an unspeakable relief to me. For "Who can dwell with perpetual burnings"?

What! thirty years of my reasoning life spent in defence of the Catholic system and twenty-six of them under the tutelage of the Society of Jesus were not enough to obliterate the impression made by Protestantism on my school-boy mind!

That were, indeed, a high testimony to the vigour of Protestantism as contrasted with Catholicism.

No, Your Eminence, it was not from Protestantism that I learnt the principle: *Securus judicat orbis terrarum.* But while holding no brief for that religion I will not deny my indebtedness to it. If there are certain other Catholic principles by which I continually judge and condemn my own conduct, their vigour in my conscience is, I think, due to the fact that with Protestants they are living forces and with Catholics they are for the most part dead formulae. The rights of authority and the rights of personality; the development of the community and the development of the individual, are not conflicting but complementary ideas. If Protestantism has forgotten one side of religious life, Roman Catholicism has forgotten the other. "The Protestant nations are sick," you say. Sick they are; but who has sickened them? Who has made their stomachs rise against a conception of authority so evil that the risk of anarchy were preferable? Who has banished the Catholic conception into complete oblivion so as to force men to choose between pure individualism and an ecclesiastical dictatorship? "The Protestant nations are sick," but the Catholic nations are dying. What has sickened those is killing these. Where the principle of unity and authority has been unduly weakened it may be restored. At all events the forces of personality are there, waiting to be organised and focussed. There is a rich chaos for creative power to work upon. The sickness is not unto death but that the glory of God may be revealed in a new life. But where authority has eliminated personality, it has preyed on its own vitals. Active co-operation in, and responsibility for, the corporate life are what constitute personality and citizenship. Of such responsibility and co-operation, the laity, then the lower clergy, finally the bishops themselves, have been deprived by a system of centralisation that leaves the Pope the sole and only responsible personality in the Church—or rather, outside and above it. The fruit is that utter decay of interest in the welfare of the body on the part of its passive and irresponsible members, of

97

which you complain in Belgium, and which is the harbinger of such a disruption as we observe in other Catholic countries. For this reason it seems to me that the Protestant nations, where religion is either a personal interest and responsibility or nothing, are more curable than Catholic nations where the laity count it virtue to throw the whole responsibility on to the clergy; the clergy, on to the bishops; the bishops, on to the Pope.

When I find Your Eminence discovering Protestantism in Dr. Döllinger, and of course in myself, I cannot help wondering whether you really know anything about Protestantism beyond the popular Catholic caricatures, which are about as discerning as the Protestant caricatures of Catholicism. If you so misunderstand what lies at your own door, are you likely to understand what is so much further removed from you? Thus I find you gravely relating on the authority of an anonymous convert from the English Church that somewhere about 1895 a bishop who had rebuked an incumbent for preaching against the divinity of Christ was notoriously disavowed by his archbishop. Any one with an elementary knowledge of the English Church and of the character and views of the archbishops of the last thirty years, would know that such a story is a tissue of the wildest improbabilities. You fancy that it requires boldness for an English clergyman to confess rather than to deny the divinity of Christ, and for a bishop to uphold him—as though it were some sort of ritualistic extravagance! Had your mind not been a *tabula rasa* ready to believe anything and everything about an utterly unknown country, you would have severely questioned this traveller's tale; you would have felt the need of inquiring carefully before making so defamatory a charge against men in such positions—against your fellow-Christians, not to say, your fellow-bishops. Who does not know this bitter type of theological convert eager to burn what he has adored and to adore what he has burned, regardless of truth, justice, and charity; who stuffs the credulous ears of his new-found brethren with what they will be most pleased to hear, most willing to believe? Is it simply from sources of that kind that you draw your inferences about so eminent a religious institution?

I can only say that if I am as sensible as ever of the limitations of the English Church, I have come more and more to understand and appreciate her manifold excellences. We have much to learn from her. If she is poor where we are rich, she is rich where we are poor. There are reasons (not the sophistical reasons of popular controversy) which forbid my return to her communion and keep me where I am, suspended mid-air. Frankly, I regret their existence, and have done my best to get over them.

All this I say lest in repudiating the charge of Protestantism which you bring against me I should seem to share Your Eminence's curious if not contemptuous estimate of Protestantism.

IX

A SUPPOSED LEADER OF MODERNISM

A S already observed, I do not complain of your summary of my views, although your italicised lines show that you read me upside down and fancy you are dealing with a plea for the crudest and most impossible individualism. I must, however, take exception to some of your incidental remarks.

In the first place, in choosing me as the representative modernist and the most authoritative exponent of that school, you do me far too great an honour, and exaggerate the importance that would attach to your refutation of me. I am not conscious of having contributed a single idea of my own to that interpretation of Catholicism. I have no claim to be an expert in criticism, nor in exegesis, nor in history, nor in philosophy, and am at best a careful follower of the results obtained by others. He who can make none, can sometimes tell good music from bad when he hears it. I think I know true metal from false by the ring. And so, with the reluctant sacrifice of many a prepossession and prejudice and soothing hope and cherished dream and darling idol, I have let myself be taught by abler and more learned men who had won the battle long before I appeared on the field. My work has been one of "vulgarisation"—of trying to illustrate and clarify for others ideas that I myself at first found strange, perplexing, and difficult.

What has pushed me into unwelcome prominence and

made me a "leader" for the journalists and their readers is simply the short-sighted indiscretion of ecclesiastical authorities. Had they acted towards me with the commonest diplomatic prudence, not to say justice and charity, at any time these two last years I should never have been heard of. Again and again they have forced me to speak when I would far rather have been silent. It is Your Eminence's Lenten Pastoral that now pushes me into print once more. Could you not have left me alone? Had you not already occasioned enough trouble for me? Nothing is more repugnant to my whole nature than that violation of the intellectual liberty of others involved in the role of the proselytiser or leader. I had rather have a white elephant than a disciple or a penitent or a convert. But even if I were a leader, to judge so diversifiecl and complex a movement as Modernism by any one of its representatives is most unfair to all the rest. I represent myself alone. Abbé Loisy is impatient of me as a dreamer and mystic. Père Laberthonnière finds me guilty of an occult scholasticism. One friend complains of my democratic, another of my conservative and aristocratic sympathies. With all due respect to the encyclical *Pascendi*, Modernists wear no uniform nor are they sworn to the defence of any system; still less of that which His Holiness has fabricated for them.

X

HIS INDIFFERENCE TO HISTORY AND DOGMA

A GAIN, you explain my aberrations by the fact that I have been "always and almost exclusively pre-occupied with the inward life of the spirit; and little, if at all, with traditional dogmatic teaching and with ecclesiastical history." Nothing could be further from the truth. My preoccupation has been almost exclusively with traditional dogmatic teaching and with the problem of reconciling it, on the one hand, with the exigencies of the inward life; and on the other, with the recent results of critical church history. As to dogmatic theology it is no boast to assert that I have nothing to learn from Rome or Louvain; for a man might say that and not say much. When I have departed from scholastic conclusions in my writings I have not done so through ignorance, as you charitably suppose, but deliberately and consciously from a sense of their ineptitude.

As to Church history it is true I am no expert. But the results about which experts are agreed have been almost my chief preoccupation, and constitute, to my mind, the essential and most characteristic feature of the problem which Modernism has to deal with. There is, I know, a certain school of mis-called Modernists for whom the historical difficulties are altogether secondary or even non-existent; whose reconstructive efforts are inspired by a sense of the inadequacy of scholastic philosophy as a vehicle of Christian thought; who feel the urgent need of

102

a religious Philosophy which shall be a faithful, experimentally verifiable analysis of the implications of religious life and action. With this school I am in profound agreement. But it is of long lineage, and not of yesterday— a revival of the pre-scholastic tradition. If to the superficial it savours of Kant, it is because both schools agree against scholasticism, and because, for that reason, much of the Kantian terminology is convenient and appropriate to the Philosophy of Action. But what the latter has in common with Kant is as old as S. Augustine, and older.

It is the historical and not the philosophical difficulty that inspires the reconstructive effort of the Modernist pure and simple. It is the irresistible facts concerning the origin and composition of the Old and New Testaments; concerning the origin of the Christian Church, of its hierarchy, its institutions, its dogmas; concerning the gradual development of the Papacy; concerning the history of religion in general—that create a difficulty against which the synthesis of scholastic theology must be and is already shattered to pieces. Gladly as I welcome the more living and flexible syntheses of the Philosophy of Action, yet so far as they ignore or evade any of these inconvenient facts or attempt to dictate to history in the old style, I have no patience with them. I will not listen to any argument *ex inconvenienti;* "facts are what they are; and their consequences will be what they will be."

Hence, though it is not in my department to bring forward or discuss these disconcerting facts, they are before my eyes in all that I write, and guide the course of my pen as so many rocks and reefs that I must get round or get over as best I may, but with which I must never come into collision. My one preoccupation is to wind my sinuous way between them so as to save all that is best in my cargo of traditional dogmatic teaching. Hence your assumption that I am little or in no wise preoccupied with traditional dogmatic teachings or with the history of the Church is as far from the truth as could well be.

XI

HIS KANTIAN PREPOSSESSIONS

NEXT, Your Eminence proceeds to show that what you call my "system" is powerfully influenced by the Protestant philosophy of Kant, with its theory of religious certitude. But surely the notion that God is attained, not by science or syllogisms, but by action and experience is considerably older than Kant. I do not suppose that Pascal or S. Augustine, or the great Catholic mystics, or S. Paul, or the fourth Gospel were influenced by Kant. To imagine that the Protestantism of my boyhood was poisoned with Kantian infiltrations is amusing for any one who knows the dry-as-dust, hard scholastic rationalism of the old-fashioned Anglican theology. One might as well seek Kant in the Pentateuch.

As far as the " method of immanence " is concerned—the method that seeks religious truth by action and not by speculation—I am able to put my finger on the exact point or moment in my experience from which my "immanentism" took its rise. In his "Rules for the Discernment of Spirits," borrowed, of course, from the great Catholic mystics, Ignatius of Loyola says, "For as consolation is contrary to desolation, so the thoughts that spring from Consolation are contrary to those that spring from Desolation." And all throughout the same rules he assumes that our thoughts and beliefs are determined by, and dependent on, our moral dispositions and affective states. Again, in his rules for making an Election and getting to know the will of God, clear vision is everywhere made to depend on the right ordering of the affections. Indeed, his Exercises are a discipline of the affections, a purification of the heart, with a view to a better knowledge of God and his will. Again, Ignatius is said to have himself used that method which he recommends to us for finding out the will of God, i.e. by observing whether a given resolution is persistently accompanied by spiritual peace or by spiritual restlessness—thus using the affective states of the soul as a means of guidance, as feelers by which we can grope our way from point to point. Then he tells us that it is God's prerogative to cause these affective states in the soul without any previous perception or knowl-edge—states which, he has already told us, give rise to inspired thoughts, and furnish a criterion of our own uninspired guesses at Divine truth.

And now, Your Eminence, if you will compare what I have written in various places from first to last on the nature and mode of Divine revelation with these princi-ples borrowed by Ignatius from the mystical tradition of the Church, you will perhaps believe me when I say that I learnt the "method of immanentism," not from Kant, nor from the Philosophy of Action, nor from Protestantism, but solely from the *Spiritual Exercises* of the Founder of the Jesuits.

He, in his turn, derived it from the great masters of that mystical method which the Encyclical *Pascendi* has swept away in the confusion of its onslaught against Modern-ism. It is to be hoped that the Book of the Exercises which has been, more than once, before the Inquisition on the charge of Protestant "illuminism" will be subjected yet once more to careful examination.

If I owe much of my Modernism to S. Thomas Aquinas, I owe still more to Ignatius Loyola. *Nova et Vetera* and *Hard Sayings* (this latter, the fragments of a projected volume on the *Spiritual Exercises*) are rightly admitted by the discern-ing to contain the substance of all my later aberrations.

They were written before I had met with or read or even heard of any of my subsequent Modernist guides and masters. These only helped me to shape and fix ideas that were formless and floating, and gradually to separate the two systems—scholastic and pre-scholastic—that were so hopelessly tangled in my mind.

It is therefore superfluous to make Kant responsible for views older than scholasticism and as old as the Gospel.

XII

HIS DARWINIAN PREPOSSESSIONS

B UT besides Kant you find another godfather for Modernism in Darwin. "It has also been influenced without doubt by the obsession, as widespread as it is unreflecting, which inclines so many clever people to apply arbitrarily and *a priori* to history, and more especially to the history of our sacred books and dogmatic beliefs, that hypothesis of evolution which, far from being a general law of human thought, is not even verified in the narrow field of the origin of animal and vegetal species."

What Your Eminence supposes to be a climax in this last clause is really an anti-climax. The idea of evolution was not derived from the Darwinian hypothesis and then extended to the mental and social evolution of man, but contrariwise. Human evolution is not an hypothesis, but a self-evident fact. I have only to look within myself to see that my mind has grown as really as my body has grown from embryo to maturity. It is not merely that I have added thought to thought, experience to experience, as one adds stones to a growing heap, each abiding unchanged in itself. As a psychologist you cannot, I am sure, accept this atomistic and mechanical notion of our mental growth. Every new ingredient changes the character of the whole compound through and through. If I use the same words today as formerly, the thoughts they evoke are necessarily richer and fuller, pregnant with new relations and connections; they have developed with the whole

mental organism in which they live and grow. The Catechism cannot mean for me at forty what it meant for me
at my first communion. Either it has come to mean more,
or it has come to mean nothing. The belt of the boy will not
girdle the man; it must either stretch or break.

And though not evident in the same way, namely, by a
moment's introspection, yet no whit less evident is the fact
of the evolution of the collective mind. It is not by mere
addition but by transformation that man passes from
savagery to civilisation. The man-eater is no longer in our
midst; he has been absorbed and transformed into something higher. The evolution of civilisation, of the collective
life and mind and sentiment, is as evident as the growth
of any individual plant or animal. It has not the slightest
connection with, or dependence upon, the Darwinian
hypothesis. The former is a matter of observation; the
latter, of inference and analogy. You cannot surely be
ignorant of the fact that the critico-historical method was
in existence and had been applied to the Sacred Scriptures
long before Darwin's time, and by men who held the
ancient belief as to the origin of species.

When you say that Modernists have approached the
history of the Bible and of dogma with a view to verify the
Darwinian hypothesis, you are true to the Encyclical
Pascendi, but not to facts. You are yourself guilty of a most
arbitrary and *a priori* judgment. Had you studied the
critics with any sort of seriousness, you could never speak
thus. That the Bible and the Church were not created
complete by a Divine *fiat*, that they have grown with the
growth of man, is not a matter of hypothesis and inference
but of observation. History catches them in the act. Those
who live on the surface of the earth may fancy it was
always thus; the geologists who dig down see that it has
grown. So as to the Bible and the Church; history has dug
down and unearthed truths unsuspected by *a priori* scholasticism. It has disclosed, not a series of types whose
genetic relation is a guess, but serial stages in the growth

of what no one denies to be one and the same individual object. It is not as though there now were several Christologies which Modernism had traced to a common root. It is simply that history shows us our one present Christology to have passed through various stages. One need only look into Petavius to see that it is so. Where does hypothesis come in? What has Darwinism got to do with it? The influence of Darwinism on Richard Simon,* the founder of Biblical Criticism, or on Petavius,+ is about as conceivable as that of Kant on Pascal or S. Augustine.

---

*Richard Simon (1638-1712). French Oratorian, widely regarded as the founder of Old Testament criticism. He was expelled from the French Oratory for his critical views (Ed.).

+ Denis Péteau (1583-1652). French Jesuit historian and theologian. Highly orthodox, but among the first to entertain the notion of doctrinal development, he influenced John Henry Newman (Ed.).

XIII

HIS INDIVIDUALIST PREPOSSESSIONS

OF your third and principal cause of Modernism I have already spoken—of "that Protestant individualism which is substituted for the Catholic conception of a teaching authority established by our Lord, and commissioned to tell us what under pain of eternal damnation we are bound to believe." Modernism, I have shown, adheres to the ancient Catholic and Apostolic conception of a teaching authority belonging to the Church as a whole, by which she is bound to preach the coming of God's Kingdom on earth, and to guide men by precept, and still more by example, to that repentance and new life without which none can enter into God's Kingdom. Modernism does not believe in the religious independence of every isolated individual; nor does it believe in the absolute subjection of all to the private will and judgment of a privileged individual who can impose theological definitions upon the rest under pain of eternal damnation.

It believes in the Church as being alone, in the full sense, Christ's Vicar upon earth, commissioned to teach what he taught and no more; and in the way that he taught it, and not otherwise; commissioned to be what he was, the revelation of a new life, the inspiration of a new hope, the communication of a new strength. The light he has commissioned her to let shine before men is not the light of science or metaphysics or even theology, but the light of that revelation of God which Christ himself was. Outside the sphere of that revelation she has no divine doctrinal authority whatever. The Kingdom and the Way as preached by Christ himself is the entire *depositum fidei*. Nothing obscure; nothing abstruse; in a sense, nothing new. A problem not for the intellect, but for the will and the heart. The Gospel is Power and not Knowledge. Strength is what men lack and not light: "To wish is present with me; but to perform I find not. Wretched man that I am who shall deliver me?"*—that is the problem which Christ came to solve and which the Church has authority to deal with in his name.

Within this sphere of her authorised teaching the Church is one and undivided and unfailing—*in necessariis unitas.* Outside it, she is divided and changeable and fallible—in *dubiis libertas.* She cannot be indifferent to theological truth, to the intellectual analysis of her own life, any more than to intellectual truth in general. She is bound to understand herself so as to direct herself as efficiently as possible. But such self-understanding is not revelation. It is no part of Christ's preaching; no condition of entering into the Kingdom of Heaven. If we live the life, it matters not that we fail in its analysis, which is always tentative and perfectible—*in dubiis libertas.* If theology has been ever a sword of division, a principle of disintegration, it is because its concepts and definitions have been confounded with that Divine revelation of which they are but the human analysis; it is because Christology has been put in the place of the living Christ and Church theory in that of the living Church; it is because that penalty of spiritual loss which is the natural and inevitable consequence of unbelief in the Gospel of the Kingdom and the Way, has been arbitrarily attached to theological error.

Men are naturally intolerant about their opinions, especially in matters rermote and uncertain where the opin-

---

* See Romans 7:18-24 (Ed.).

111

ions are more wholly the children and creatures of their own will and judgment. It is for religion and morality to assuage, not to foster, this egotistic ferocity and to counsel liberty in open questions. But let hell be the penalty of theological error; let man's natural intolerance receive a divine consecration and blessing, and the result can only be what it has been—hatred, persecution, division and subdivision. Liberty, and not compulsion, is the only way to secure a healthy progress towards that free theological unity which, though not a necessity, is a primary desideratum for the well-being of the Church. Had no more ever been imposed as of necessity than what Christ imposed—the Kingdom, the Way, the Life; had faith in the living personality of Christ not been confounded with intellectual assent to Christological speculations, the whole world might have been Christian by this time. But as it is, the Gospel with all its theological paraphernalia easily gets tangled in the brain before it reaches the heart. Not till the Church is content with unity in necessaries, not till she grants liberty in uncertainties, will she attain unity either in these or in those.

In the propagation of the Gospel, in the work of revelation, the Church possesses the same sort of spiritual authority as Christ himself. And so far as her appointed officials speak really, and not merely by a sort of legal fiction, in her name, their voice is hers. They are not merely her "delegates,", for in the measure that they truly represent her they are not distinct from her, but are part of the very Church which speaks, and co-depositaries of her spiritual authority. A delegate does not identify himself with the message he carries. Outside the sphere of her divine mission—in matters of science and metaphysics and economics and politics they are as other men, only perhaps with a deeper obligation of fidelity in the quest of truth.

XIV

MODERNISM AND SCIENTIFIC FREEDOM

"THE doctrines condemned by the Encyclical," Your Eminence goes on to say, "are such as to repel the Christian conscience by their bare mention." Naturally enough. For atheism, agnosticism, and materialism are among the reckless charges there laid against Modernism. But the strange thing is that such repulsive conclusions should issue from such attractive principles: "There is something seductive in the Modernist *tendencies* which makes an impression on certain minds otherwise attached to the faith of their baptism. Whence comes this? How is it that Modernism has such an attraction for the young?"

It is indeed a serious problem. If the young are with us, we have only to wait. A generation more and the whole world will be with us. The young are with us because, as you imply, they belong to the dawning and not to the declining age. The two deepest characteristics of the new order are the scientific spirit and the democratic movement—a new conception of truth and a new conception of authority and government.

So far as Modernism is, in these respects, with the age and the Encyclical against it, the young are drawn to the former and repelled by the latter. You therefore proceed to show that the Encyclical in no way interferes with scientific liberty, and that, even if Democracy be at all permissible in politics, yet the Church is by Divine and positive institution an absolute monarchy or spiritual dictatorship, and must be taken or left as such.

I have already noted (p. 45) that though Modernism is not synonymous with modern thought, yet the condemnation of the former may entail that of the latter. The condemnation of a synthesis may fall on one or both of the united terms or on their amalgamation.

The assertion that the Encyclical *Pascendi* interferes with scientific liberty is, you tell us, a calumnious accusation of an infidel and hostile press. You appeal in proof to what Belgian Catholics have done for science—though the proof demands that you should confine your appeal to what they have done with approval since the Encyclical of last September; for it is the effects of the Encyclical that are in question.

You tell us that "the representatives of the philosophical and theological schools of our universities, and of our free faculties and seminaries and religious congregations have unanimously and spontaneously declared and proved, by a document signed by each of them, that the Pope has, by his courageous Encyclical, saved the Faith and protected science. Ah! this spontaneity and unanimity! If it were only a little less it would be so much more! Being what it is, it is just nothing at all. What would be the lot of the unfortunate professor, or teacher, or seminarian, or student, or monk, or nun, who, by refusing to sign such a declaration, were to be exposed to all the petty persecutions prescribed by the Encyclical in question, and eagerly put in execution by all the bigotry, jealousy, ambition, and sycophancy now let loose on the Church to her shame and humiliation? Do we not all know, as well as Your Eminence, how these unanimous and spontaneous expressions of adhesion and satisfaction are, if not ordered, yet at least "expected" of every bishop under pain of Rome's displeasure—and how promptly they have been forthcoming? Have we not learnt and blushed over the secret of the spontaneous unanimity of the French episcopate on certain recent occasions—over the double

114

insincerity of those who could exact and accept, and of those who could proffer, a lip-service as to whose value not even the simplest are deceived?

Once more, let me remind you that an engineered uniformity has nothing to do with spiritual unity; that to be significant, the concurrence of witnesses must be absolutely free and independent; that a man is not free who is threatened with persecution, calumny, disgrace, and starvation. All that this signed declaration proves is that Belgian Catholics are thoroughly drilled and centralised; that they are passive and plastic as putty in the hands of their priests. You think this a symptom of life; I think it a harbinger of death and decay. I know your drill-sergeants too well to have any doubt about it. It is only a corpse that will obey like a corpse; only a stick that will obey like a stick. I am therefore not impressed by your signed declaration; nor am I so sure as Your Eminence that Belgium has not its little muster of timid Modernists meeting in some upper chamber for fear of the Jews. It is hard to believe that the youth of the country are "attracted" towards Modernism and yet rest impotently in their velleity; that so much tendency never arrives at any result. It must be, I think, that your "Vigilance Committee" is not quite properly organised, or has not yet grown expert in methods of detection and espionage.

Those who, like Your Eminence, believe that the object of Faith is a revealed theology, a body of divinely guaranteed terms and definitions and statements, final and valid for all ages and nations, are quite consistent in holding that the Encyclical, far from interfering with scientific truth and liberty, is their friend and protector. For the solidarity of theology with other sciences and with the totality of knowledge is not to be denied. If God's word vouches for any one science that science must be the rule and criterion of all the rest. To be under its control is not slavery but liberty—liberty from error. Nay, it must be a cause of rapid and fruitful progression. While an unaided astronomy or geology or history is delayed and weakened by uncertainties, that which derives were it only three or four fixed and infallible truths, from Scripture or Tradition, has a solid foundation to build upon, and builds itself up rapidly and securely. Such for centuries was the supposed relation of Catholic science to revelation. Such it is still for Your Eminence and for the Encyclical *Pascendi*. Such it must necessarily be if scientific propositions form, however implicitly, part of the substance of Divine Revelation. But if they do not; if revelation be not theology, the bondage of science to the fallible theological conceptions of a past age is a bondage indeed, an insuperable obstacle to progress.

Can we say, on looking back over the history of its development, that the control of science by a revealed theology has been a stimulus and not an obstacle? that since it has thrown off that control it has languished? that it has declined steadily from the sixteenth to the twentieth century—more especially in Protestant countries? Can we say that what Your Eminence would call "the teaching of the Church" enforced under all sorts of pains and penalties, temporal and eternal, has notably hastened and facilitated the discovery of truth as to the nature and history of the world and of man? Is it not just in the name of revelation that the whole authority of the Church over conscience has been brought to bear against one science after another, so as, if possible, to strangle them in their birth? If the Church had had her way, if Reason had not refused to listen to her outside the narrow limits of her teaching commission, our scientific conceptions today would be those of the Bible. We should believe that the world was flat or concave, and not spherical; or that if spherical, there were no antipodes; that the stars were hung out like lamps night by night; that the sun swept round the earth day by day; that man was created only six thousand years ago; that fossils were created just as and where we find them; that eclipses and meteors were miraculous portents; that the multiplicity of languages was a preternatural phenomenon; that all races derived from the three sons of Noe; that all animal species had existed in one spot and were represented in Noe's ark; that the whole world had been submerged and drained dry again in a couple of years. We should still be burning old women on the charge of the evil eye or of intercourse with the devil; we should be treating epilepsy, hysteria, and insanity as diabolic possession; we should be using prayer and exorcism instead of medicine, surgery, and hygiene; we should be ringing consecrated bells against storm-demons and earth-shakers; the chemist would be a magician; the money-lender an excommunicate.

The men who first challenged these positions were condemned and energetically opposed in the name of revelation as heretics and blasphemers. Had they been free-thinkers, such opposition had been far less effectual. But they were believers who accepted the current confusion between revelation and theology; who knew nothing of the distinction (forced on us so slowly) between the experiential and the intellectual values of the sacred writings; or who, at most, tried vainly to deny the solidarity of theology with other sciences, and to separate the scientific from the theological teaching of the Bible. And, therefore, just because of their belief, their conscience was enlisted against their reason and their senses; and their energy was paralysed by the illusion of an imaginary contradiction between truth and truth, between revelation and science. It was not purely the fear of ecclesiastical tyrants, but also the fear of God and of a perplexed conscience that made men, like Galileo, retract a known truth in deference to what they believed to be a revealed truth. Thus it was that for centuries the scientific efforts of Catholics were checked and frustrated by theology posing as revelation. As soon as that yoke was shaken off, science rushed forward by leaps and bounds.

But all that, you will say, is past history; nor were

117

Protestants any better than Catholics in those days of general obscurantism. Now everything is changed. The Church puts no fetters on physics or physiology, or geology, or astronomy. We are free as the wind; we are abreast and ahead of freethinkers in all these subjects.

Yes, but who won you that freedom and at what cost? Was it the Church and the theologians, or was it those whom theology opposed and persecuted, and by whom it was beaten back again and again and finally reduced to a sullen ungracious silence? Is it due to a change of principle on the part of theology, or to a loss of power? On the part of Protestants it is largely due to a change of principle. But when we turn to the Encyclical *Pascendi*, we find the old principle reasserted in its crudest form; we find the scientific and historic infallibility of the Bible affirmed under pain of making God a liar. We are bound down to all the scientific and historic implications of scripture and defined dogma; we are told that science must be ruled by scholastic theology and that such rule is for its benefit and protection. The principle is not changed. Moreover, it is to be applied vigorously just to that science which is the most characteristic and important of our day—to the scientific criticism of history. Theology, learning nothing from her past defeats, is to contest this new field on the old lines, with the old weapons; by accusations of blasphemy and heresy; by delations and inquisitions and petty persecutions. The very tone of the sophistical attack on the critico-historical method—now violent and injurious; now supercilious and satirical—echoes that of the official refutations of the new astronomy of Galileo.

When, therefore, you assure the youth of Belgium that the Encyclical leaves scientific liberty intact, you must be thinking of the natural sciences against which its principles are now simply helpless, and which theology has wisely learned to leave alone; and you must be forgetting the one science upon which the whole Modernist controversy turns and which is condemned along with Modernism. Can you deny that the criticism of the Bible and of Church history is a science? Can you deny that this science—the most fruitful and important of our age—is condemned root and branch by the Pope's Encyclical? Can you deny that the whole document is a reassertion of the principle by which freedom of all science is inevitably condemned? If the Church now had her way, if she had the control of all education in her hands, what would be today the prospects of historical science—of history controlled by the conclusions and presuppositions of the *Summa Theologica* of S. Thomas? It is, of course, because you sincerely believe in a divinely revealed infallible history that you can persuade yourself that the control of revelation must further and not hinder true criticism. But I doubt if the youth of Belgium will long share Your Eminence's persuasion.

When you appeal to the superior efficiency of the Catholic, as opposed to the non-Catholic, schools and colleges of Belgium, one would gladly see in this a conclusive proof of the Church's awakened zeal for general education, as such, and apart from all ecclesiastical self-interest. But who does not see that even Catholic parents will not trust their children to the Church schools unless these can secure their temporal interests as well as, or even more efficiently than, the State schools? Everywhere it is the same. Competition and the law of self-preservation force the clergy to an activity which they rarely exhibit in the absence of such competition. For this reason I cannot regard your argument as by any means proving your point. General education does not create the atmosphere in which a "revealed theology" can best flourish. Theologians have always felt it, and have accordingly looked with suspicion on general education as a danger to what they suppose to be Faith.

But, living in evil times, they must perforce go with them, or go out of them; and they choose the lesser disadvantage. I speak, however, of the dying, not of the rising generation of clergy.

Do I then mean to admit that the Church is hostile to science or to any human interest? God forbid! I only mean that theologians and ecclesiastics are not the Church; that revelation is not theology; that since there is a relation of solidarity between theology and every other science, the Church in proving herself fallible in science proves herself fallible in theology. Since belief in a revealed theology issues in scientific error, that belief is not true. Theology is human; Revelation is Divine. Revelation is a supernaturally imparted experience of realities—an experience that utters itself spontaneously in imaginative popular non-scientific form; theology is the natural, tentative, fallible analysis of that experience. The Church's divine commission is to teach and propagate a new life, a new love, a new hope, a new spirit, and not the analysis of these experiences. Her theology is true and helpful just in the measure that it grows out of and ever returns to the collective religious experience of those who live the life and breathe the hope of the Gospel as preached by Jesus Christ.

XV

MODERNISM AND POPULAR GOVERNMENT

THE other attraction that Modernism exercises over the youth of Belgium is its conception of ecclesiastical government and authority. Modernism, apparently in the wake of Dr. Döllinger, has been led astray by the principles of J. J. Rousseau and of "the rights of man." It is a child of the French Revolution. The youth of Belgium are unfortunately saturated with these same modern notions of parliamentary government, and are consequently out of sympathy with the idea of the Church as a divinely established absolute monarchy whose power is gathered into the hands of a single irresponsible individual.

That you should identify the Catholic and historical view of the constitution of the Church with the principle of government by numerical majorities is not more surprising than that you should hail a disciple of Rousseau in a deeply conservative thinker like "the apostate Döllinger"—a man who lived his whole life in the pages of ecclesiastical history, and whose protest against papal absolutism was in name of past facts and not of present philosophy. I am not going to qualify such criticism, for I could not do so without some indignation.

Let me state simply that the mind of the Church to which the bishops in council bear witness is not that of a numerical majority, nor even of the total number; but is the corporate mind of the whole community—as different a thing as is any organism from the sum total of its separated parts; as different as is water from two parts of hydrogen and one of oxygen; as different as is a stone building from a heap of stones.

For political and practical purposes, the fiction that the will and opinion of the majority is also that of the minority is necessary. But to settle matters of truth, and especially of religious truth, by a majority-vote was a precedent invented by the Vatican Council. Till that time, moral unanimity was required as the authorisation of ecumenical decrees. For in what sense could that be the mind of the Church, of the Christian *orbis terrarum*, which was contrary to the mind of such a portion of it as any appreciable number of bishops would represent? It is not a practical question of making and forming, but of discovering and declaring the universal belief.

To turn a Council into a theological debating club where most votes carry the day, was possible only for men who were dead to the organic character of the Church, and who, under the influence of revolutionary and Napoleonic conceptions, had come to regard it as an artificial structure.

The faith of the Church is not that of each individual, be he Pope or layman. In each, the Christian spirit manifests itself in some new and particular aspect, never twice the same. No one can say "I am tradition," "I am Christianity." It is by the social interchange and comparison of these ceaseless and varying manifestations that a corporate mind is formed and developed which serves as a standard to waken, guide, and stimulate the development of each several soul. Here is the advantage of an institutional Church, within whose limits the experiences of multitudes and generations are brought together and unified for the general good. And it is to this end that the Church needs to be organised hierarchically, so as to bring to one focus the countless rays of her spiritual illumination, and to distribute the contributions of the rich and able to the utmost advantage of the poor and needy. In no sense are the bishops in council the delegates of their flocks. This pastoral metaphor is the root of much evil. The bishop is part of the same organism as his flock—nay, he is the principal part. He and they are one moral personality and not two. He is not outside and above them; nor are they outside and above him. He and they have but one corporate mind and will. It is of that corporate mind that he is the representative—not of his own separate mind nor of theirs. Nor, again, is the Pope the delegate of the universal Church as of a distinct moral personality. As the first among his brother bishops, he is the principal representative, not of his own individual mind, but of the corporate mind of the Church. As bishop of the principal see to which Christians flock from all parts, he is (as Irenaeus says) in touch with the general mind, which in ordinary cases can be learnt more expeditiously through him.

It was from history and not from Rousseau that Dr. Döllinger learnt the true Catholic tradition of authority. You imply that I go still further in the direction of Rousseau. But I can attach no meaning whatever to your words. You say, "It is this conception of authority that Döllinger would apply to the bishops in council. But Tyrrell applies it alike to the bishops and to the faithful ... of the Christian community." You mean apparently that as Döllinger views the bishops as mere delegates, so I view the laity also as mere delegates. Delegates of whom, in the name of Reason? There cannot be a *processus infinitus* in delegation. With Rousseau the people is sovereign and not delegate.

Possibly you mean that as Dr. Döllinger makes the bishops mere delegates of the faithful, so I make the Pope the mere delegate of the bishops. But so to put the Pope under the bishops would be to take him out of their rank and file just as much as to set him over them. It is this mechanical separation of the united members of a single organism with one life, one mind, one will, that I object to.

For your "bishops in union with the Pope," I would put, "the Pope as united with the bishops and the bishops as united with the Church." Till I can attach some meaning to your remark I must regard it as a rhetorical flourish. At all events, I am as unconscious of differing in this point from Dr. Döllinger as I am of agreeing with Rousseau.

I have neither the inclination nor the ability to embark in a discussion as to the best form of government. But, on the one hand, a system which commits the most difficult and complex problems to the vote of the majority, that is, of the least educated and competent, seems to me sheer madness; as much as it would be to decide theological controversies by popular ballot. As to the daily experiences and natural exigencies of soul and body; as to immediate appearances and impressions, in contradistinction to reflections and inferences, all men are equally competent to judge. Outside that sphere, wisdom is with the few and fewer, and not with the many. On the other hand, an absolute monarchy is tolerable only on the impossible supposition of a prince who is infallible in wisdom, goodness, and power. As we know that institution in history, it is something essentially evil and altogether anti-Christian. It has sometimes tried to save itself from this latter imputation by the doctrine of the Divine Right of Kings and the claim to a more or less miraculous grace and guidance guaranteed to the monarch by the King of Kings. Under this cover its worst atrocities have been committed. But even in its best manifestations it has been incompatible with that conception of personal dignity and responsibility which is the best fruit of Christianity. To be delivered from one's petty individualism; to live out of oneself and enter into the corporate life and interests of the community to which we belong, it is necessary that we should be at least allowed to share in its action and further its aims; that we should feel ourselves responsible for it in some degree; that we should feel honoured in its honour and shamed in its shame. If we have no responsi-

124

bility; if our sole duty is to obey passively and blindly in the service of ends that are unknown to us—ends, nominally public, but usually those of a selfish bureaucratic clique; if we are little better than witless forces to be disposed of by our rulers, we cease to be persons, and the boundaries of our own separate individuality become those of our interests.

And the modern interpretation of the papacy as an absolute spiritual monarchy has had precisely these results. It tends to make, not only of the laity and the lower clergy, but even of the bishops, so many wooden marionettes whose strings are pulled in the office of the Pope's Secretary of State. As a spiritual absolutism it is a far more deadly enemy of personality than any political absolutism ever has been, or could ever possibly be. Though outwardly a slave, an Epictetus can be inwardly a personality. He can, without rebuke from his conscience and his religion, feel himself as a man responsible for humanity; he can feel that the concerns of society are his concerns. He can remain a free citizen in the City of God.

But that right of citizenship is taken explicitly from the Catholic layman and priest by the Encyclical *Pascendi*. It is left to the bishops nominally, and for very shame, lest the stones should cry out. The layman is told that he has no active part whatever in the life and movement of the Church, except as a blindly obedient force at the absolute irresponsible disposition of the Pope. It is not his business to think, to understand, to feel, to suggest, but simply to obey.

Nothing seemed stranger to me on first coming to live among Roman Catholics, and still more among priests and clerics, than their extraordinary supine indifference as to the deeper and more universal interests of their religion; as to the bearing of current movements and events and opinions on the fortunes of their Church. It was not that their zeal was first directed, but that it was so exclusively directed, to their own little personal and party concerns; and that they regarded it as a dangerous eccentricity to manifest a responsible interest in "the whole state of Christ's Church militant here on earth." The rare exceptions were, for the most part, recruits from the Church of England or elsewhere. In this respect the Roman Catholic clergy seem peculiar among professional men, who, as a rule, are keenly interested in the general progress of their science, art, or business. Yet the reason is fairly evident. If there is nothing more to know, or than can be readily known by application to headquarters; if all power and responsibility are in the hands of one man; if in spite of blunders and abuses God has promised success and triumph; if it is distrust and presumption to trouble oneself about the course of events; if we are minors and not persons, slaves and not free citizens, is it possible to be interested in more than the actual task committed to us by authority and to be performed in a spirit of blind obedience? And may not this be the reason why the buried and forgotten interpretation of Catholicism, unearthed by the Modernists, offers some attraction to the youth of Belgium as suggesting that their religion is a great world-cause for which they are personally responsible and in which they can co-operate actively with all the best energies of their minds and hearts? May it not be the reason why you ransack the libraries of their seniors in vain search for a New Testament or a Roman Missal or a shelf devoted to religious literature?

But, whatever the disadvantages of absolute monarchy in general—and they are in some ways increased where the miraculous powers of the ruler justify a complete resignation of all responsibility into his hands—you will tell us that we have no choice in the matter: "The Church as a supernatural society is essentially of positive and external institution and must be accepted by its members in the shape in which it has been organised by its Divine Founder. It is for Christ himself to dictate his will to us." That is, the Church has not grown and developed from within, like a natural social organism, in virtue of an immanent vital principle. It was created instantaneously as an absolute monarchy, with its Pope, bishops, priests, deacons, dogmas, sacraments, institutions, by the *Fiat* of the historical Christ. Like the Adam of Genesis it sprang from the dust full-formed and mature in mind and body. As I have already had occasion to remark, Your Eminence ignores the existence of the most characteristic and important science of the day—the critico-historical science on whose application to the sacred writings and traditions of the Church the whole Modernist controversy turns. You somewhat beg the question when you refute Modernism with the assumption that it is already refuted, and that this abrupt creation of the present Roman ecclesiastical system by the *Fiat* of Christ may be taken for granted. Far from being self-evident, this view becomes daily more and more untenable in the light of historical criticism—a light which no doubt you suppose you may disregard as having been successfully extinguished by the Encyclical. It is a view that will find no new recruits and whose last defenders will die out in a generation or two. To anchor the Church to it, is to anchor a boat to a whale. The whale sinks and the boat sinks with it. Its historical worth will be as incredible in a few years as that of the story of Eve and the serpent, or that of the universal deluge.

Every new insight we get into the history of Christian origins is unfavourable to this view of the abrupt and complete creation of the Catholic Churcl by Christ "according to the flesh"; to the view that S. Peter had the same official self-consciousness as Pius X; that he felt himself bishop of bishops and ruled over his brethren as an absolute monarch. It is not a question of explaining a series of admittedly different species by the "hypothesis" of genetic connection; but of observing a series of stages through which an individual institution, undeniably the same, has actually passed. Everything points more and more inevitably to the conclusion that what Christ founded was not the hierarchic Church but the little body of missionary brethren, which subsequently, under the guidance of Christ's Spirit, organised itself into the Catholic Church; that he did not directly commission some of them to teach and rule over the rest; but commissioned all of them equally to go and teach all nations and prepare them by the baptism of repentance and by a new life for the instant coming of the Kingdom of God upon earth. And such a view, far from belittling the dignity of the Church or denying its divine institution, exalts it and sets its claims on a far firmer basis than that supposed to be furnished by the distorted and most disputable exegesis of half a dozen critically dubious texts.

If it comes to texts, it seems to me that the defenders of absolutism forget, when convenient, the promise of Christ to be with and in his Church to the end, to send her his indwelling Spirit to guide her into all truth; they forget that he identified himself with the mystical Body of those who were filled with his own spirit and kindled with his own fire. Do not such expressions as " He that heareth you heareth me," " Whatsoever ye shall bind on earth shall be bound in Heaven," etc., justify the Modernist in regarding the Catholic Church as a Divine institution built up by Christ ever immanent in the body of his followers? Do they not allow him, without violence to history, to speak of the historic Christ as having laid its foundation in that apostolic body of missioners out of which, as its root, it subsequently grew under the guidance of God's Spirit? Is it not the old question between the static and dynamic views of God's operation? Have we yet to learn that he works as a sage, not as a wizard; by process, not by cataclysm? That Catholicism so originated is not a matter of hypothesis but of observation. The most tortuous wrigglings of exegesis will not save the ultramontane thesis of the new theology.

Yet since wheat and tares have grown side by side in the same field, we cannot at once conclude that the absolute monarchy of the Pope, such as the majority at the Vatican Council would fain have defined and established it, is the work of Christ immanent in the Church. He cannot contradict himself; he can unfold but he cannot gainsay the principles of his Gospel. He who restored to us our personality and spiritual liberty cannot rob us of our rights as free citizens in the Kingdom of God. We are not in much doubt as to his ideals of a spiritual government. His disciples are his friends and not his slaves just because they are sharers of his designs, freely co-operating, not blindly obeying; actively following, not passively driven— "The servant knoweth not what his master doeth." Will you contend that these words were addressed to bishops alone or, rather, to "the bishops in union with the Pope"? It is a hardy contention. He tells us that "the rulers of the nations domineer over them, and those who are greater among them exercise authority over them. But not so with you. Let him who would be greater be your servant, and him who would be first become your minister. For the Son of man came not to be served but to serve." Can you doubt for a moment that the kind of government that is here condemned and forbidden to the Church is the government of the Roman Caesar, whose claims, principles, and methods were taken over bodily by the Popes of the Middle Ages and by their successors, who still, with a curious irony, style themselves at once "bishop of bishops" and "servant of the servants of God"? Easier to squeeze blood from a stone, than the spirit of absolutism from the Spirit of Christ. Tares may grow among wheat, but not from the same roots.

It is not merely historical criticism that refuses to view the absolutism of the modern papacy as the personal institution of Christ. Can you—no, you cannot pretend that the rigidly conservative and traditional Churches of the East are Protestant or individualist, or under the revolutionary influence of Rousseau. Yet while they bear concordant testimony to the ancient primacy of the Roman bishop among his brethren; to his duty of leadership by good example and spiritual authority, they, as concordantly, deny his claim to be a bishop over bishops, and to rule his brethren with an absolute, irresponsible juridical authority.

That which attracts the youth of Belgium to the Modernist conception of Church government is therefore something which it has in common, not with Rousseau, but with the Gospel of Jesus Christ and with the ancient Catholic tradition of East and West confirmed by the results of that critico-historical method which the Encyclical has condemned.

*   *   *   *   *

So much, then, Your Eminence, by way of criticism of your Lenten Pastoral. It is a lengthy reply to so brief a document; but the shortest text may sometimes demand the bulkiest commentary. In a million ways one may miss the mark of truth. It is the easy work of an instant. But to hit it fair and square takes time and trouble; and a lifetime may be too short to refute the errors crowded into half a page of reckless indictment.

I would fain think I had taken a fugitive document too seriously; that it had been hastily drawn up in the odd intervals of a busy morning or at the fag-end of a weary day. But the facts that you have demanded and obtained for it the special approval of the Holy Father, and are about to give it the permanence and universal publicity of a brochure, forbid me to do so, and force me to believe that you yourself regard it as an adequate and deliberate utterance of your best thoughts and deepest convictions.

To me it has been a matter of renewed and profound discouragement to find so much confusion of ideas, so much misapprehension of history, of the significance of certain movements, of the positions of certain persons, on the part of one whom popular rumour had pointed out to me as perhaps one of the most brilliant lights of the Sacred College—nay, even as possibly the orient star that might one day rise yet higher to dispel the darkness of our present state. That faint flicker of hope has been rudely and completely extinguished.

XVI

ONE ASPECT OF MODERNISM

B UT before I take my leave of Your Eminence, let me, simply in my own name, and neither as a pretended leader of Modernism nor as claiming any special comprehension of so complex a movement, say what Modernism meant for me, and how I understood it.

The term "Modernist" has been used in a sufficient variety of senses to cause a considerable amount of confusion. If not invented, it has, at least, been established by the Encyclical *Pascendi* as the prejudicial designation of a party in the Roman Catholic Church. But already it is accepted as the designation of liberal Christians of all sorts, and bids fair to supplant the older term "liberal," which, as standing for a political as well as a religious principle, is somewhat less exact. "Modernist" as opposed to "modern" means the insistence on modernity as a principle. It means the acknowledgment on the part of religion of the rights of modern thought; of the need of effecting a synthesis, not between the old and new indiscriminately, but between what, after due criticism, is found to be valid in the old and in the new. Its opposite is Medievalism, which, as a fact, is only the synthesis effected between the Christian faith and the culture of the late Middle Ages, but which erroneously supposes itself to be of apostolic antiquity; which denies that the work of synthesis is necessary and must endure as long as man's intellectual, moral, and social evolution endures; which

132

therefore makes the medieval expression of Catholicism its primitive and its final expression.

Medievalism is an absolute, Modernism a relative term. The former will always stand for the same ideas and institutions; the meaning of the latter slides on with the times. If we must have a sect-name, we might have a worse than one that stands for life and movement as against stagnation and death; for the Catholicism that is of every age as against the sectarianism that is of one.

A good deal of the force of the Encyclical as an appeal to the Christian sense is due to its ambiguous use of the term Modernist.

It professes to be describing those Roman Catholics who believe in this principle of "Modernism," and who are confident that a synthesis between faith and the established results of criticism is possible without damage to either. But, in fact, it describes as Modernists those Catholics also who possess no such confidence; who consider that criticism is fatal to Catholicism and to its principal beliefs and institutions, who ridicule such syntheses as utopian, and who, in many cases, are among the most active opponents—official or unofficial—of "Modernism." In short, it describes as "Modernists" all those professed Roman Catholics who accept the results of criticism, however those results may tell upon their faith, whether disastrously or otherwise. Thus it cleverly lays every "Modernist" open to the suspicion of being an Unitarian or an atheist or an agnostic; it brands them all alike as hypocrites and pretenders. Unfortunately there are, and there always have been, such men in the Church even on the Chair of Peter; and that, long before the days of criticism. Scepticism is not modern, nor is atheism, nor hypocrisy. Let us, then, keep the word "Modernist" to designate those who believe in the Roman Catholic Church as firmly as medievalists do; but whose deeper faith is not frightened but stimulated by the assured results of modern criticism. For, as it is belief in the living Christ that

133

makes a Christian, and not any particular Christology, so what makes a Catholic is not this or that abstract theory of the Church, but a belief in the historical Catholic community as the living outgrowth of the apostolic mission. No one who has lost faith in the mission and destiny of the Roman Church and in the advantage of being identified with it is a Roman Catholic.

To believe in the living historical Catholic community means to believe that by its corporate life and labour it is slowly realising the ideas and ends in whose service it was founded; that through many fluctuations and errors and deviations and recoveries and reactions it is gradually shaping itself into a more efficient institution for the spiritual and moral development of individuals and societies; that by its continuity and extension it is the collective subject of a vast experience of good and evil, of truth and fallacy, and of a slow but sure process of reflection on the same; that if it advances laboriously and imperceptibly it is because its evolution, like that of nature, is the result of so vast, so costly and even so cruel an experience, and because the contributions of individual effort are opposed tooth and nail until their right to survive and conquer has overcome almost every conceivable objection. One's belief in the Church as the organ of religion is to some extent one's belief in the laws of collective psychology, which are the laws of nature, which are the laws of God.

I have laboured heavily at this idea in the first chapters of *Scylla and Charybdis* and will here say no more. In this belief in the living organism of the Church, Modernist and Medievalist are at one. They are both Catholics whatever their theoretical analysis of Catholicism; both have a right to be in the Church. As far as one does not believe that the Church is slowly working out an ever truer and more fruitful religion; as far as he views the whole process as barren, idle, unmeaning, "a tale told by an idiot full of sound and fury but signifying nothing," he does not believe in the Church and is not a Catholic.

But the Modernist is a Catholic with a difference. What is this difference?

The difference is that whereas the Medievalist regards the expression of Catholicism formed by the synthesis between faith and the general culture of the thirteenth century, as primitive and as practically final and exhaustive, the Modernist denies the possibility of such finality and holds that the task is unending just because the process of culture is unending. Hence the new historico-scientific methods and their results, the new social and political ideas and institutions, being irreconcilable with the medieval synthesis, seem to the Medievalist irreconcilable with what he considers to be the primitive final and perfect expression of Catholicism. The old synthesis has been perhaps modified at the Councils of Trent and the Vatican; but only along the same lines and categories, and by way of defining more closely its opposition to post-medieval culture. The Modernist is no blind worshipper of present culture. He knows it is a medley of good and evil, and needs careful criticism and discrimination. But he believes that, on the whole, it stands for gain rather than loss; and that its new and true values must be absorbed into the Catholic organism if the latter is to live.

If he believes in the Church as a Catholic, as a man he believes in humanity; he believes in the world. To regard the world outside the Church as God-forsaken; to deny that God works and reveals himself in human history, that he is in and with mankind in all its struggles against evil and ignorance and degradation, that he is the primary author of all intellectual, aesthetic, moral, social, and political progress, seems to the Modernist the most subtle and dangerous form of atheism.

Nay, of the two, his faith in the world is more fundamental than his faith in the Church—in the world of which it is written, "God so loved the world that he gave his only begotten Son." For he who sits at meat is greater than he who serves; and the Church, like her Master, is sent for the

135

service of the world; to serve it, not to rule over it, or trample on it, or despise it. If she has something to teach it, she has much to learn from it. It is the living whole of which she is but an organic part; and the whole is greater than even its most vital organ. The Modernist loves the Church for the sake of the world and humanity; which means that he loves humanity more, as the fuller and all-inclusive revelation of God. The Manichean dualism that opposes the church to the world, as light to darkness, is to him a compendium of many heresies. Any barrier that hinders their free interchange of benefits is impoverishing to both alike. Each must absorb the quickening forces of the other under pain of a monstrous and lop-sided development.

Again, whereas the Medievalist, with his mechanical and static idea of ecclesiastical infallibility, canonises the entire medieval synthesis indiscriminately; the Modernist, with his dynamical idea of a process that will infallibly work out right in the end; with his conception of our highest truth as ever alloyed with error, of our highest good as ever alloyed with evil, is one who discriminates and qualifies, who distrusts absolutism of every sort.

He does not view the essence of Christianity as consisting of one or two simple principles given from the first and abiding unchanged beneath a bewildering mass of meaningless and mischievous encrustations. Its essence is continually being built up by the expansion and application of these normative principles; by their combination with all that is good and true in the process of human development. It consists not merely in the leaven but in the whole mass that is leavened and christianised, and that grows in bulk from age to age. So far he agrees with the Medievalist against the Protestant. But he does not believe that the process stopped with the thirteenth century and is, therefore, truer to the Catholic principle.

For him, however, it is a double process of good and evil; of false and true. He recognises, what the reformers could not recognise with their dim historical light, that the tares were sown almost contemporaneously with the wheat; and are always being sown; that if the wheat has grown, the tares have also grown even from the Apostolic age—from the first pious tamperings with the Gospel text; that there has been a development not only of good but of evil principles, not only of truths but of errors, not only of the leaven of the Gospel but of the leaven of hypocrisy. He sees that in every generation some tare or another ripens and betrays its true character and needs to be uprooted; that there are epochs when a perfect harvest of such tares demands a sort of revolution—a ruthless thrusting in of the sickle of criticism, a binding in bundles and burning of noxious weeds. He recognises in the recent developments of the Roman-law conception of ecclesiastical authority on the one side, ancl on the other in the recent results of biblical and historical criticism and of social and political developments, the signs of such a crisis in the life of the Church. His is no blind Philistinism that would raze the Church to the ground and run up a smart up-to-date structure on the old site. He holds firmly that nothing which has, on a large scale and for a long period, both lived and given life can be destroyed without irreparable loss and impoverishment. His sole effort is to separate the perishable from the imperishable elements in all such cases; to change as little, to preserve as much, as truth and truthfulness will permit.

Alive to all abuses and errors connected with dogmas and institutions, he is not less alive to the services they have rendered, to the principles they have imperfectly expressed. Christ-worship, saint-worship, miracles, sacraments, dogma, theology, uniformity, ritual, priesthood, sacrifice, papacy, infallibility, nay, Medievalism itself, all stand for so many attempts to satisfy the religious requirements of human nature.

Whatever is mechanical, gross, unhistorical, or decadent must be so removed as to save those values by which they have lived in spite of their evident limitations. If the marriage of Christian principles with the sane principles and elements of growing civilisation has been fruitful of true developments of the Catholic idea, their marriage with the unhealthy and evil elements of the same has produced spurious developments, in which, however, the nobler strain must be recognised and purified. Even things so utterly evil as persecution and inquisition have been not merely approved by good men, but approved as right, because they were the perverse and stupid application of the undoubted truth that the destroyer of souls is a greater danger to the public than a murderer; that temporal death is a lesser evil than spiritual. No immorality could have lived and thriven unless it had perversely appealed to conscience under some appearance of morality. We must not empty out the baby with the bath. We must save the apparent morality if we would reveal the full deformity of what it covered and what will else return in the same guise.

And so, for the Modernist, even the errors, sins, and follies of the past are valuable experiences which the Church is all the wiser and deeper and richer for having passed through and beyond. In this, the same law governs the formation of collective as of individual character. Virtues that have not been driven home by hard struggle lie light on the soul's surface; the storm that rocks the tree roots it. It is by the experimental method that Nature gropes her way to what is more useful, more true to life's laws. Catholicism is a great experimentation in religion; a quest of the fullest and most perfect expression of Christianity. Medievalism, in the eyes of the Modernist, is a necessary experiment which must be worked out to its extremest and bitterest consequences if the Church is to realise inwardly and comprehensively a truer, deeper, richer notion of liberty and authority, of faith and orthodoxy, of revelation and theology, of growth and identity, than were possible otherwise. Thus it is that God in history is ever judging the world, gathering the wheat into his barn and burning the chaff with fire unquenchable. For ourselves, with omnipotence and omniscience at our disposal, we should have arranged things differently; we should have saved all the waste and woe of this tedious experimental process; we should have created an immutably perfect Church by the *fiat* of our will. But God's ways and thoughts are not as ours, nor can we wonder if he works as slowly and wastefully in the Kingdom of Grace as in the Kingdom of Nature. The argument from what we ourselves should have done to what God must therefore have done is the principal basis of the ultramontane Church-theory; but it is somewhat shaken by the consideration of what God has actually done and does daily.

Finally, the Modernist demands, not greater freedom, but absolute freedom for science in the widest sense of the term. He will not have it fettered except by its own laws and methods and by the experience which is its subject-matter. He will not allow even theology to be tied down to any revealed and stereotyped statements, but only to the religious experiences of which certain statements are the spontaneous self-chosen, but at most symbolic, expressions. Such experiences are the substance of revelation; the inspired statements are but its classical and primitive symbols, and cannot be treated as premises for deduction.

Science for him is one general system dealing with all experience and trying to arrange it into a single synthesis of the understanding. As a theologian, he takes account of spiritual and supernatural experiences as part of the totality of experience; he considers the religions of mankind; the religion of Israel, the religion of Jesus and his apostles, the religion of the Catholic community—all, as so much experience. He considers the spiritual forces and tendencies and sentiments that have embodied themselves in the history, institutions and doctrines of the Roman Catholic Church and in the lives and actions of her children, and which are revealed in defeat as well as in victory, in false as well as in true developments. And from such consideration, he arrives progressively at a better idea of the essence and aim of Catholicism and at a truer criterion by which to shape the course of its future developments.

Modernism therefore has nothing to do with that sort of more educated and temporising ultramontanism that shrinks from an inopportune pressing of principles which the world has unfortunately outgrown; that loves to rub shoulders cautiously with science and democracy; that strives to express itself moderately and grammatically; that would make a change of circumstances and opportunities pass for a more tolerant spirit; and that is usually rewarded for its pains by finding itself between the hammer and the anvil.

Modernism does not seek to modify this or that tenet or institution It is an all-pervading principle affecting the whole of Catholicism from end to end with its distinction between the divine and the human element; the spirit and the embodiment; the permanent and the variable. If it is a heresy at all, it is "the compendium of all heresies."

Thus, if we speak of it as a movement or tendency guided by certain principles and methods which it is prepared to follow with a certain blind faith whithersoever they may lead, it admits of a fairly clear description. But if by Modernism we mean a finished theological system like that of the scholastics with a definite and final answer to every theological problem, and if I am asked what is to be the upshot of these methods and principles, what is to be the modernist theology of Christ and the sacraments and the scriptures and so forth, I have a perfect right to answer "I do not know"—just as a socialist has a perfect right to say that he does not know what socialism is; that he cannot provide a finished theory of it; cannot see below the horizon; cannot define an idea that is slowly working itself into consciousness and is necessarily incoherent and elusive in its earlier self-utterances. He knows that the whole world is in labour; but he knows what is going, better than what is coming. As against existing social institutions and ideas, which are clearly definable because they are played out and dead, he is dumb and easily convicted of folly, just because he is feeling after something living that is coming to birth through a series of uncouth embryonic developments. But if by socialism we mean not the theory or idea but the process, tendency, or movement which binds millions of men together for a common end and for a work that is directly constructive, and indirectly destructive, socialism is quite definite and concrete.

And the same is to be said of "Modernism" so far as it stands for the living assembly of Modernists and not for the idea or end, as yet obscure but most real and active, that inspires and binds them together. In the abstract, Medievalism is definable because it is dead; Modernism is not so, because it is living and growing. A system that perforce ignores all the results of man's mental, moral and social development since the thirteenth century is naturally more simple and definite than one that not only tries to assimilate those results, but that holds its conclusions as merely provisional in view of further and yet further results, that has abandoned the idea of finality and recognised the work of synthesis as an abiding and unending duty.

When any statement or formulation of experience is accepted as exhaustive it soon comes to usurp the place of experience, to be the X or Y that does duty for it in its absence. Mistaking the symbol for the reality, the formula for the thing, we cease to be pressed by the inadequacy of the formula, as we are pressed by it when the two together are present to our consciousness. We can easily fit certain predicates to Christ or to the Church when these are mere names and concepts for us, but not so easily when what is present to our consciousness is the living Christ and the living Church. For then we are ever sensible of the inadequacy of our predications—of the need of adding aspect to aspect, and relation to relation; of adjusting and re-adjusting and correcting and improving.

The Modernist therefore denies the scholastic's right to challenge him for definitions and conclusions that are ever in the making and never made. And if it be objected that at that rate he has no message for the millions—for the poor and the simple—he replies, first, that their need of definite statements would not justify false and premature statements or a pretence of finality where none existed. Secondly, that the issue is not between popular religion and modernist theology, but between scholastic theology and modernist theology, both of which are the scientific, non-popular justification of popular Catholic belief and practice. What we preach to the poor is not theology, but revelation—the inspired and simple expression of those experiences which theology translates into the technical language of philosophical systems.

Finally, we reply that the scholastic system, for all its meretricious simplicity, is fully as unintelligible to the crowds as the immanental or the pragmatist system. For does any serious man believe that its theological expressions concerning the Trinity or the Hypostatic Union or Transubstantiation which Medievalists teach the faithful to repeat, correspond to or evoke any coherent concep-tions in their understandings? Do we not know that theologians themselves when pressed close are found to be dealing with words and words only? Has Your Emi-nence any clearly different concepts answering to the words "generation" and "procession" in the Athanasian Creed; or to such expressions as "spiritual presence" or "wholly in the whole and wholly in each part" or "three persons in one nature" or "one person in two natures"? If you think you have, is it not only because you think that other people have ? No, Your Eminence, when we preach to the people what Christ preached—the coming of God's Kingdom, the baptism of repentance and a new life—we feed them with bread; when we preach scholasticism, we feed them with words and wind: "For this cause many among you are sick and weakly, and many sleep."

But it would be wrong to suppose that because the growing ideas of modernist theology are necessarily incomplete and indefinable they are therefore worthless. For man, truth is an unending process of adequation, not a finished result. His understanding and analysis can never do more than outline the growing masses of his experience. The inadequacy of his conceptions is not merely quantitative; they are not a mathematical half or quarter or tenth of the whole. Each addition changes the quality, the truth-colour, of all that has gone before, as each new ingredient changes the quality of a chemical compound. Still, what is acquired is acquired, though it be transformed and transcended by subsequent acquisitions. The grub survives in the moth, the foetus in the adult; and so of the succesive expressions which the same reality or experience creates for itself in the human mind. Each expresses the same thing; each begets its follower and is begotten by its predecessor. Furthermore, each is of permanent value in determining the direction of the whole process which cannot be rightly understood or criticised except from the study and comparison of its several phases.

When therefore it is a question of preaching Christianity to others, or of living it himself, the Modernist apprehends and presents it under the same inspired and imaginative symbols as the Medievalist. When it is a question of giving scientific intellectual expression to the experiences for which those symbols stand, when it is a question between theologians, he refuses to regard any theology as final or to predict what form it may assume in its endeavours to unify religious experience with future accumulations of general experience. It will be tied by no statements, by no graven inscriptions; only by the facts of experience for which such statements stand, and by the laws of the mind.

Hence, because a Modernist's theology, i.e. his intellectual construction of Catholicism, is living and growng, it cannot be presented with the clearness and definiteness of a theology that is finished and dead, and that is impervious to the quickening influence of contemporary culture.

Further, it is perfectly obvious that modernist theologians will not agree among themselves as do those who learn, almost by rote, a system imposed upon them in the name of authority, by an appeal to their conscience rather than to their reason; who are supported by this uniformity, this spurious semblance of unanimity, in their confident defence of the same, and who fancy that what is held so firmly and generally must be self-evident to others if not to themselves. If faith works miracles, faith in the faith of others is more mighty still. It can clothe the naked with a garment of glory, admired by all and seen by none.

XVII

OTHER ASPECTS OF MODERNISM

THIS, Your Eminence, is Modernism as it seems to me from the point of view of my own life-long interests and preoccupations since my first boyish struggles with the ponderous Bishop Butler up to the present moment. If the desire to make religion a living truth for living minds be Modernism, I was a Modernist in my boyhood, and in my earliest and most ultramontane days, and during the long years when I rummaged patiently for the Holy Grail among the dustheaps of scholasticism under the direction of men whose infectious self-assurance was not easy to withstand.

It is the aspect of Modernism interesting to one whom you describe, with just a touch of superciliousness, as "anxious above all things to retain in the Church such of our contemporaries as are disconcerted by the noisy assertions of unbelievers who, sometimes in the name of natural sciences, sometimes in that of historical criticism, would pass off their own philosophical prejudices and hypothetical conjectures as assured conclusions of science in conflict with our Faith."

Your Eminence, if I have been dealing with such facile dupes, I have been dealing for the most part, as you know very well, with those who have had every advantage that a seminary education can afford; who have sought guidance earnestly from their official teachers, and have sought it in vain; who have asked what they should think, and

145

have been told not to think at all; to close their books and their brains and to pray against the temptations of the devil. For the purpose of the givers, no wiser advice could be given.

But Catholicism is more than a theology; nor is it merely the intellectual side of Medievalism that comes into conflict with so many-sided and complex a phenomenon as modern culture and civilisation. Hence Modernism, which hopes and works for the solution of all these conflicts, presents, not in each of its representatives (as the Encyclical imagines), but in all of them together, an endless variety of aspects. All are agreed that the medieval world is dead; that the Church cannot be tied to its corpse and live. But each views the great sphere of the world, whether old or new, from his own side, and none compasses it altogether. Hence the task of synthesis is undoubtedly far vaster and more difficult than any one of us realises. Looking at his own corner of it, he may have moments of sanguine hope. Could he see all, he might well despair. Yet the spontaneous division of labour which has made the world can remake it. We have not set ourselves freely to this collective task or chosen our places. We are pushed on, organised and directed by the universal forces that govern the progress of humanity, by the ideals that are struggling to realise themselves in a not very distant future. Our interpretation of those obscure forces and ideals is sure to be faulty to some degree. Hardly any such movement in history—not the Protestant reform, nor the Jesuit reform, nor the Franciscan reform, nor even the Christian reform—has followed the lines foreseen and desired by its first adherents. Such men have been always the half-blinded instruments of a Power with far wider plans than theirs. Their partial bondage to an impossible Past has been the very condition of their serviceableness as mediating channels by which the values of that Past are transmitted to a Future which to them would have seemed as impossible, and altogether undesirable.

What we desire and labour for is the revival of decadent Roman Catholicism; and this, in what we believe to be the truest interests of religion. Even if our belief were mistaken, our labour would not be in vain. The spirit that lives in us and moves us and unites us cannot fail of its ends which are greater than ours. It has already passed sentence of death on Medievalism, which has been tried experimentally, weighed in the balance, and found wanting. And now Modernism is to be put on its trial; and of that experiment we are the forced instruments. Its issue we cannot foresee. We know that like every experiment it will make for truth, whether by success or failure. Is the ecclesiastical organism strong enough to exclude the new ideas altogether and live; or is it still strong enough to assimilate them; or is it so weak as to be killed by the effort of assimilation? Who shall say? God's world will go on, and no labour in its cause shall be thrown away.

XVIII

POSSIBLE TRANSFORMATIONS OF
MODERNISM

THE Modernist's belief in the Church is, I have said, subject to and dependent on his belief in the world and humanity. There are not two Gods but one, who works and reveals himself both in the great whole and in the included part. I speak of the world that "God so loved." The world of which it is said "Woe to the world" and "Love not the world" is inside as well as outside the Church, and in its most repulsive because hypocritical form.

But as our belief in the Church, so also our belief in the World must be discriminating; it must be a faith in the meaning and value of a process rather than in the finality of results, however useful, already reached by it. Modernists would not be mortal if the difficulties of their actual position, the persecution and annoyance to which they are subjected by their domestic enemies, did not concentrate their criticism on the Church rather than on the Age, and incline them to see in the latter nothing but what they miss and desire to find in the former. This were merely to set up one Philistinism against another.

If the repressive measures of the Encyclical succeed at all, it will be in this unexpected way. They may kill Modernism by transforming it into something much more violent and dangerous than Modernism; much more akin to the movement of wholesale revolt in the sixteenth century. Without being a prophet or the son of a prophet,

148

I seem to see very unwelcome signs of such an eventuality. There were no doubt many quiet thinkers in the eighteenth century who hoped that better ideas of liberty and the rights of man would slowly permeate the general mind and effect a peaceful reform in social and political institutions. But while they were thinking and philosophising, unheeded as idle dreamers by those in authority, the people, exasperated by oppression, had seized on their half-comprehended principles and given them a crude practical application as unwelcome to philosophers as to kings; an application that reacted in favour of tyranny and threw back the cause of liberty by more than a century. To-day while the "Modernism of the study" is not only unheeded but actively repressed by the Vatican bureaucracy, the modern spirit, felt rather than understood, idolised rather than criticised, has penetrated and inflamed with enthusiasm large numbers of the Catholic clergy and laity, and roused a spirit of revolt that may be ill to reckon with. It is a revolt far less of the enslaved intellect than of the moral and religious sense violated by the cynically irreligious and self-interested opposition of the Vatican bureaucracy to all the best aspirations of civilised humanity; by its indifference to every cause but that of its own aggrandisement and domination; above all, by the unworthy Machiavellian methods through which it would secure its ends.

Popes come and go; but this overgrown bureaucracy that exploits the papacy abides unchanged as to its spirit, its methods, its ends. Here we have a vast multitude of men for whom the centralisation of the Church at Rome means money and position; whose private interest it is to push the papal claims to their utmost extreme. With them, the Pope can do everything; against them he can do nothing. They are the channel of his communication with the Church, and nothing can pass from one to the other but through them and in the form most suited to their collective advantage. It is against this compact army of offcials

149

that the Catholic conscience is beginning to rise in indignation.

For a time the personal integrity of the reigning Pontiff kept revolt in abeyance. But since the Montagnini* revelations and other incidents have, to our shame, made public the methods and principles of our ecclesiastical government, the duty of a loyal, but now futile, silence gives place to that of protest and repudiation. Far from being rebuked, the Nuncio and his substitute have been honoured and promoted. And Rome imagines that she can still claim unqualified respect and obedience; that no apology or explanation is needed; that all her sins must be overlooked and forgiven in deference to her high official position!

This is to press an abstract truth to its extremity. We should distinguish the office from the man; and be able to reverence the former however unworthy its bearer. But psychology puts a limit; and a moment comes when the strongest reverence is too weak to hold indignation in check, or when it is even a duty to withhold any sort of reverence that might seem to associate us with principles and methods that we find morally objectionable. We are men first and priests afterwards; and things may reach— if they have not already reached—such a pass that to be a priest or even a bishop one must cease to be a man and become a passive tool in irresponsible and possibly unscrupulous hands. Quite apart from the evils that may actually result from it, the position itself is as profoundly immoral as that of the members of a secret society sworn to the blindfold service of ends into whose nature they may not inquire.

Little wonder, therefore, if all that is earnest and generous and Christian among the younger clergy is ready for

---

* Mgr Carlo Montagnini was papal chargé d'affaires in France during the complicated and abrasive period of the Separation of Church and State in the first decade of the twentieth century. In 1906 he was expelled from France and his files were seized. These files revealed the Vatican in a rather poor light (Ed.).

revolt; if men refuse to receive, as the mandates of God, orders engineered by the army of career-hunters who supply the Pope with the falsified information necessary for their own godless ends. Little wonder if this quickly gathering force of instinctive indignation is impatient of the moderating control of carefully balanced syntheses, elaborated by quiet students far removed from that centre of actual conflict where ideas are embodied in men and the battle is between persons and interests rather than thoughts. The condemnation and persecution of such students has, at once, added fuel to the fire of this anger and convinced the more practical-minded men of the futility of fighting vested interests with the frail weapons of reason. Strong movements, like strong men, have need to be narrow-minded and one-sided; they cannot afford to weaken their resolution by "thinking too precisely on the event"; they must often face the risk, nay, the certainty, of loss for the sake of a balance of gain. To the reformers in question, Socialism with all the crudities and shortcomings and anti-Christianism is more Christian, more akin to the Gospel, with its "enthusiasm for humanity," than the cold-hearted cynical ecclesiasticism to which it stands opposed. Their moral and religious revolt against the latter bids fair to drive them blindly into the arms of the former. If they cannot civilise the Church, they will evangelise the world.

Such is the spirit that Pope Pius X has raised, especially in Italy, by his attempts to lay the ghost of Modernism for ever; and this new ghost will be still harder to lay. Those Modernists who hitherto kept the younger and hotter heads in control and bade them have faith in the leavening power of truth, in the quiet permeation of ideas, in the scythe of Time that would soon mow down the grey-headed votaries of a dead past, must now perhaps stand aside and witness helplessly a conflagration in which their own careful syntheses and constructions will be burnt up, and which may throw back the realisation of their hopes for generations, if not for ever. Though God is not in the earthquake, the whirlwind or the fire, but in the gentle breeze, yet he rules over and controls them as perhaps the necessary harbingers of the still small voice that is to follow. These violent experiments may well be essential to a more satisfactory apprehension of truths that are as yet immature.

Frankly, I cannot regard as a true development of Catholicism a movement which leaves any one of its values aside in order to insist on others that have been neglected. Such one-sided insistence may, as I have said, be a necessary condition of future development. But it is none the less one-sided; and such a movement when, like Protestantism, it becomes schismatic and distinct from Catholicism, is something infinitely poorer and thinner. Yet even such schisms have undoubtedly served the cause of Christianity by keeping alive certain aspects of its truth that else had perished, and so preparing the way for some future reintegration. It may well be then that to carry out the integral programme of Modernism simultaneously in all its parts is an impracticable ideal, something inherently impossible; that it is only by a series of concentrated one-sided efforts, mutually corrective and complementary, that its aim can be slowly realised. Our ways and thoughts are not always those of God and Nature, and often owe their superior brilliancy to their fallacious simplicity.

But Modernism, as I understand it, professes belief in the Church as well as in the Age; in the possibility of a synthesis which shall be for the enrichment of both, the impoverishment of neither. To sacrifice either to the other is to depart, rightly or wrongly, from the Modernist programme.

In accordance with that programme, our faith in the Age, its ideas, tendencies, and institutions, must not exclude, must rather stimulate a ceaseless effort of criticism and discernment. Here too wheat and tares are mingled inextricably, and the very tares demand careful study. Here too every evil lives under some semblance of good, and every lie thrives by its honest face; nor may we hastily uproot abuses that are as yet inseparable from honest uses. We must learn to look on the history of the world as we look upon that of the Church; to see there an experimental search after the conditions of life in general; as here, a search after those of the spiritual side of life in particular; to regard failures no less than successes as instrumental in the work of evolution; to learn, not merely from the present results, but from the whole process by which the past has grown into the present on its way to the future; to seek a rule of action from the direction of the process, rather than from any momentary phase which dissolves while we look at it into something different, and leaves us guideless and sceptical.

A credulous enthusiastic faith in the thoughts and tendencies of today may be excusable and necessary as a revolt against a similar faith in those of the thirteenth century. But the similarity is there, and the difference is only between philistine and philistine.

Your Eminence, if Faith is of the very essence of Modernism, Criticism is no less essential, nay, it is but a quality of its Faith, a proof of its vigour and purity. Faith in the divine governance and direction first, of the great world of human life, which God so loves, and in which he dwells and works and suffers, and dies and rises again in ceaseless process; and then, of the Church which he has set in the heart of the world to leaven it with the leaven of the Gospel and to safeguard the deepest and most central interest of humanity—but a Faith so firm that it can afford to be fearlessly and pitilessly critical in its certainty that the bitterest truths are the most wholesome, that the deadliest poison is that of a spurious optimism which drowses our senses with its opiates of flattery and illusion.

It is indeed no ordinary Faith that can discern, whether in the Church or in the world, a growing substance of imperishable truth under the accidents and appearances of so much pretence, unreality, and downright imposture; that can trust to the immortal forces of life in the face of such signs of decay and disintegration; that can see, between the leaves, blossoms and fruits that come and go aimlessly, the steady development of the hidden branches that bear them. Such is the faith of Modernism; and those who, like Your Eminence, cannot share it, owe it at least the tribute of respect due to every great and noble illusion that has led its victims to forget themselves, to sacrifice their peace and prosperity, never wholly in vain, for the supposed cause of God in Humanity.

XIX

THE DEATH-AGONY OF MEDIEVALISM

IF then, for the greater secrecy of its own designs, the
Roman bureaucracy has once more "set its foot upon
the light," it has little reason for self-gratulation. It has
extinguished a flame only to raise a conflagration whose
consequences are incalculable. Sooner or later, if the Church
goes on, the inevitable question will have to be faced again
and at a greater disadvantage for the delay. It is the old
story of the Sibylline Books. Perhaps the offer that has
been so rudely rejected is the last; perhaps even now the
Kingdom of God has been taken from you and committed
to a Faith no longer found in Israel. What has happened
once may happen again. You rest your fatalistic and
enervating assurance on divine promises not half so clear
and strong as those on which Judaism justly relied for its
perpetuity—promises that are always conditional, and
are cancelled by the presumption that trespasses on them;
that casts itself headlong from pinnacles and despises the
natural laws of safety.

If you are quite wrong in regarding me as the embodiment of more than a fractional aspect of so diversified and
complex a manifestation as Modernism, I am quite right
in viewing Your Eminence as embodying adequately that
scholastic simplification of Catholicism which you find so
well adapted to the comprehension of first communicants. In addressing one medievalist I am addressing all.

Let me then plead with you in the name of Religion and

155

Humanity, to face the inevitable facts of your situation. The world which it is your mission to evangelise has already slipped from your grasp. You have nothing to hold it by. Neither its intellectual nor its ethical, nor its social, nor its political ideas are yours. If it is interested in you at all, it is only as in a medieval ruin where no sane man would seek shelter in a storm. It has passed you by long since, and if now it throws a momentary backward glance at you, it is because of the clamorous pretensions of Modernism to march with the age, and your clamorous outcry against those pretensions. "What is this brawl," it asks, "in the household of death?"

The times are in labour with a new world whose characteristics are hard to divine from the obscure manifestations that herald its advent. But they will certainly not be those of the thirteenth or the sixteenth century to which you would tie the cause of Catholic Christianity finally and for ever.

Do you imagine that the coming world will listen to a Church that has identified itself not only with the philosophy and theology of a dead past, but with the moral standards and conceptions which the line of casuists represented by Gury* have developed to their profoundly immoral consequences? Will men long be content to estimate human acts from the outside as separate atoms or entities torn from their living context in the personality that gives them their unique unclassifiable character? with the attempt to apply the forms and methods of the *forum externum* to the infinite complexity of the inward life? Will they go on admiring a casuistry of evasion whose pride it is to whittle away duty to its lowest and meanest terms ?

Will they bear with the mechanical profit-and-loss as-

---

*Jean Pierre Gury (1801-66). French Jesuit moral theologian who was an influential exponent of the casuistic method in moral theology (Ed.).

ceticism represented by Rodriguez;* the foe of the older
Catholic mysticism and of all healthy expansive spiritual-
ity; the parent of a servile and pharisaical scrupulosity—
of all that morbid self-concentrated introspection which
destroys the fresh spontaneity of the divine spirit in man;
which is ever totting up merits and dissecting intentions
and keeping the left hand assiduously informed of the
doings of the right?

Will they accept a quasi-physical or metaphysical idea
of a Grace whose light is hidden under a bushel from the
eyes of men, which has no necessary bearing on ethical
character, and may even vary inversely with morality?
Will they listen to you when you teach them implicitly to
look down on the natural virtues—truth, courage, honesty, industry, fidelity, humanity—as supernaturally
worthless or indifferent, as proceeding merely from man,
and not from God in man? Or when you insist on the
superiority of passive over active virtues—of those which
limit rather than constitute character; which make absolute and irresponsible government free to play what
pranks it pleases ?

Will they continue to see the highest fruit of Christianity
in a sanctity that is measured by ecstasies, automatising,
stigmata, and all the symptoms of psychic disorder; or in
far-fetched austerities that have nothing to do with self-
government or self-sacrifice, but proceed from a Manichean
dualism or from a belief in a vindictive God appeased by
profitless and purely retrospective pain and suffering?
Will they consent to give to a conditional and limited
virtue like obedience the supreme honour due only to
such absolute virtues as truth and charity; to make it cover
a multitude of sins against one and the other, and suffer
the coward conscience to shift its burden on to other

---

* Alfonso Rodríguez (1538-1616). Spanish Jesuit ascetical and spiritual
writer. His *Practice of Perfection and of Christian Virtues* (1609) was
influential both inside and outside the Society of Jesus (Ed.).

shoulders and drowse away into lethargy and paralysis?

Will they be held back to your medieval notions of authority; to your methods of government which assume a state of chronic antagonism between rulers and ruled, whose appeal is to fear and self-interest; whose maxim is: Divide and reign?

Above all, do you imagine that by allying yourselves against the people with all the decrepit props of absolutism, crowned or discrowned, you will be able to stand against that social revolution which is pressing towards us with the slow irresistible might of an advancing glacier, avenging itself mercilessly on every obstruction? Do you think that, because this or that or every present socialist theory is wild or impracticable, all this imperfect thought and groping tendency will come to nothing; that the obscure idea which inspires them will never take flesh and dwell among us; that the scholastic Encyclicals of Leo XIII have solved the problem or even grasped superficially the simplest of its terms?

Your Eminence, the opposition between these medieval notions (of which I have adduced but a few typical specimens) and those of the coming world is not one that can be adjusted by the most ingenious patchings and compromises. It lies in a contrariety of principles from which the opposing notions spring, and by which they are animated and bound together. On the one side, the category of mechanism—government by machinery; truth by machinery; prayer by machinery; grace and salvation by machinery. On the other, the category of life and growth and spiritual unity. Which is the Catholic and Christian principle I need not discuss again.

But if tying the Church to medieval notions has reduced her to her present state of spiritual impotence, to tie her as blindly to the notions of today would be only to postpone the date of her disaster. The axe must go to the root of the tree—to this radical lie that has branched into a whole system of lies each needed for the support of the rest.

What, then, is this *proto-pseudos*, this *idée-mère*, this *erreur fondamentale* of Medievalism which has been tried in the balance for so many centuries and at last found wanting; which has run up a debt to truth that threatens the Church of today with insolvency? It is (as I am weary of repeating) the confusion of faith with orthodoxy; of revelation with theology. It is the notion of the Church as an organ of intellectual enlightenment; as a schoolmistress commissioned to teach us by rote a divinely revealed metaphysics and physics and ethics and sociology and economics and politics and history. You say that the Church has at least an indirect mission in these matters; and so do I. But you mean that she holds some revealed statements and premisses in these several sciences with which the rest must be squared. I mean that she is guardian of that spirit of truth and truthfulness; of patience and self-abnegation, and of all those affective dispositions of the heart with which science must be pursued for the glory of God in the good of mankind. I mean that her mission is to the heart and not to the head; that the Gospel is primarily power and strength and inspiration for the will; that it convinces by ideals, not by ideas; by the revelation of a coming kingdom and a new life set before the imaginative vision and kindling a fire of enthusiasm.

This is the eternal and immutable value of the Christian revelation of which the Church, commissioned to transmit and spread the sacred fire, is the depositary. It is thus and not as a body of ideas that she exercises a spiritual influence, not a despotic mastery, over the development of man's mind and the progress of human life.

Nothing, as I have said, is more self-evident than the ceaseless development of human thought and knowledge, and of every human institution dependent on thought and knowledge. What do not grow in man are the elementary passions and emotions, the spiritual driving-forces that set his mind and hands to work, and that are stimulated by ends and motives, by the appearance or the reality of Good. It is to these that the Gospel appeals by the ideal that took flesh and lived in the personality of Jesus Christ. It is from him that the corrupt self-seeking Will of man learns to labour disinterestedly and devotedly for the Kingdom of God on earth; to battle against every sort of error and ignorance; to investigate the roots of social evil and sin and misery; to feed the hungry and clothe the naked and heal the sick and instruct the ignorant.

But all this growth of knowledge and understanding is man's own work and no part of the revelation that has inspired his mental labours, and directed [them] to the Kingdom of God in man.

Catholicism stands not merely for the leaven of the Gospel, but for all that has been, or is in process of being leavened by it; not merely for the fire, but for all that it has set burning. It is within the Church where the experiences of so many peoples and so many centuries are united and compressed and forced into harmony, that the Gospel-spirit seeks experimentally to embody itself in the best form of external religious institution. Catholicism is neither the unchanging spirit nor the growing organisation, but the two together.

In her own way the Church has everything to do with the universal interests of mankind, with the development of human thought and life. She can never be indifferent to any sort of truth, theological or ethical or scientific or social. The cause of progress is the cause of God's kingdom. Yet her duty is not to interfere with but to protect the freedom and autonomy of these sciences; not to dictate premisses or conclusions, but to cultivate the spirit of truth and truthfulness, of intellectual humility and self-abnegation; to secure the moral dispositions that condition the fruitfulness of mental labour. Again it is a question of the difference between juridical and spiritual authority.

The Church in each age will rightly have her own opinions, her premisses and conclusions, like the rest of the world; but let her not tie herself to them or confound them with that revelation and message to the heart which is the substance of her divine commission; let her not impose them on the conscience "under pain of eternal damnation"—*in necessariis unitas; in dubiis libertas.* She is troubled about many things that are expedient, whereas but one thing is needful.

How can the world imagine that you have faith in God, that you believe sincerely in the harmony of revelation and science, when it sees you so manifestly afraid of criticism, afraid of the light, afraid of liberty, afraid of outspokenness and moral courage; when it sees the Encyclical placing all its hopes in the repression of knowledge, in the paralysis of mental activity, in the revival of those inquisitorial methods, unchristian and unmanly, that have done more to dishonour religion and scandalise the world than all the enemies of the Church put together?

XX

THE MORAL ROOT OF THE CONFLICT

YOUR Eminence, the principle that divides Medievalism from Modernism is at the root moral rather than intellectual; a question less of truth than of truthfulness, inward and outward—of a rigorous honesty with oneself that makes a man ask continually: Is this what I really do think, or only what I think that I think? or think that I ought to think? or think that others think? that teaches him intellectual modesty and humility and detachment; that restrains his impatient appetite for the comfort and self-complacency of a certitude (natural or supernatural) which entitles him to be contemptuous, arrogant and dogmatic towards those who differ from him.

It is a question of respect for the liberty of other minds; of a scrupulous veracity that will make no concession to the exigencies of edification, nor deem any loose statement justifiable in support of what is believed to be a revealed truth; nor imagine that such pious tamperings with the truth can ever be God-pleasing and meritorious.

Diplomacy is not the best school of veracity; though seeing that the relations of diplomatists are frankly those of chess-players trying to outwit and deceive one another, it may be maintained that such professional sharp-dealing is consistent with personal truthfulness. Nor again are the spirit and methods of absolute and irresponsible government usually favourable to outspokenness and candour.

Repression is met by stealthy evasion; distrust and duplicity in the rulers evoke the same qualities in the subjects. We are prepared for these miseries in the secular state whose ends are avowedly temporal and earthly. But we do not expect to find the Church of Christ governed by methods that are associated with the most cynical forms of oriental despotism and that make it impossible to trust the word of an ecclesiastical official who may be speaking, for all we know, only from his "communicable knowledge" or in this capacity or that capacity, or under this or that mental restriction, or may even be boldly lying with all the licence of a diplomatist—and all this in the name of Christ and in the cause of Christianity.

And a still deeper and older source of this untruthul spirit is the initial error (already touched on), the *idée-mère* of Medievalism, that gives the authority of divine revelation to a mass of untenable historical and scientific statements that belong merely to the primitive expression of revelation. One knows how even a single false premiss will develop into a vast and complex system of falsehoods the further one pushes the argument that it vitiates. Bind men's consciences, then, to a whole host of such premisses; forbid them to criticise them; force them to bring the results of their observation and reasoning into accord with them; compel them to defend such premisses against all gainsayers, against all texts and facts and documents that may be adduced against them, and the result must be just what it has been—a profound inward scepticism begotten of the apparent conflict between truth and truth; an absence of anything that deserves the name of intellectual conviction; an inability to understand or respect such conviction in others; a readiness to think black is white when so commanded; a habit of controversial chicanery and dishonesty that strikes at the very root of candour and truthfulness.

Add to this the decadent and enervating casuistry of the pulpit and confessional which is never weary of insisting

on the merely venial character of untruthfulness and of
relegating veracity to the very inferior rank of natural or
pagan virtues, and we have a sufficient explanation of that
all-permeating mendacity which is the most alarming and
desperate symptom of the present ecclesiastical crisis.

Those Modernists who put their trust in the spread of
truth, will labour in vain unless they first labour for the
spread of truthfulness; nor are they faithful to their "method
of immanentism" if they hope for an intellectual before a
moral reform. What would it avail to sweep the accumu-
lated dust and cobwebs of centuries out of the house of
God; to purge our liturgy of fables and legends; to make
a bonfire of our falsified histories, our forged decretals,
our spurious relics; to clear off the mountainous debts to
truth and candour incurred by our ancestors in the supposed interests of edification; what would it avail to
exterminate these swarming legions of lies, if we still keep
the spirit that breeds them? In a generation or two, the
house swept and garnished would be infested as before.
The only infallible guardian of truth is the spirit of truthfulness. Not till the world learns to look to Rome as the
home of truthfulness and straight dealing, will it ever look
to her as the citadel of truth. It will never believe that the
spirit of Machiavellian craft and diplomacy is the spirit of
Christ. "Can the same fountain send forth bitter waters
and sweet?"

XXI

CONCLUSION

YOUR Eminence, will you never take heart of grace and boldly throw open the doors and windows of your great medieval cathedral, and let the light of a new day strike into its darkest corners and the fresh wind of Heaven blow through its mouldy cloisters?

In spite of the clamorous contradiction of my reason and common sense, I cannot even yet bring myself to believe that it is too late; I cannot resign myself to the thought that what has been built up by the labour of so many centuries, at the cost of so much suffering and sorrow, is now doomed to destruction as a mere encumbrance. I will not face, because I can so hardly resist, the impression that the rich and varied experience in good and evil of so notable a section of humanity as has been gathered within its walls is to be as water poured out on the ground, or as a column of vapour dispersed in the broad air. I cannot, or at least I will not, believe that the persecuted minority who in every generation have striven loyally against the overwhelming forces of ecclesiastical corruption and abuse have laboured in vain, or that we shall never reap in joy the harvest they have sown in tears. Can it be that the Church which so many legions of martyrs, saints, thinkers and scholars have enriched with their very best, with their heart's blood and their spirit's anguish, is to fall the prey of a selfish and godless bureaucracy? that the gates of hell so long resisted are at last to

165

prevail against her and shut her up into medieval darkness for ever? Is she to have neither lot nor part in this new world that is struggling painfully to the birth and so sorely needs that quickening inspiration of divine breath which it was her mission to impart?

Shall the once-thronged city lie deserted and the Queen of the Nations be made a widow and the streets of Zion mourn because there are none to come to her solemnities, because her gates are thrown down and her priests in tears and her virgins in rags and she herself oppressed with bitterness? Shall her gold be tarnished and her fine colours faded and the stones of her sanctuary lie heaped at the street corners, and all this because she has let her sucklings perish for thirst, and refused the bread of life to her little ones—to the starving millions of our modern civilisation who wander harassed and worried as sheep having no shepherd; or because for the scarlet rags of a secular splendour departed long since and for ever she has forgotten her true glory, and has walled herself round with stone and iron, and narrowed the borders of her tent, and from a world-embracing religion as wide as the heart of Christ has shrivelled herself up to a waspish sect glorying as none other in her rigidity and exclusiveness?

Is this what Catholicism has come to—so grand a name for so mean a thing? Is this the religion of all humanity and of the whole man; of the classes and the masses; of the Greek and the barbarian; of the university and the slum; neither above the lowest intelligence nor beneath the highest; neither a burden to the weak nor an offence to the strong; the religion not so much of all "sensible men"—for all are not sensible, as of all honest men—for all can be and are naturally honest; a religion unencumbered and unentangled with contingent and perishable values, free as an arrow in its flight straight home to the universal conscience of humanity?

All this we had a right to look for in the Church of Rome, the nursing-mother of European civilisation. And what do we find? Are her breasts dry? Are her hands empty? Can she do nothing for us—nothing at all?

Your Eminence, I know it right well, yet I will not believe it. My faith in the Church is, in its very different way, as blind as your own. It is part of my faith in humanity whose prospects seem not less desperate. The very word "Catholic" is music to my ears, and summons before my eyes the outstretched all-embracing arms of him who died for the whole *orbis terarrum*. If the Roman Church still holds me it is because, in spite of the narrow sectarian spirit that has so long oppressed her, she cannot deny her fundamental principles; because, as a fact, she stands for the oldest and widest body of corporate Christian experience; for the closest approximation, so far attained, to the still far-distant ideal of a Catholic religion.

The very paganisms with which the Church is reproached assure me that all the streams of religious tradition from the most ancient times and the most distant quarters of the earth have met in her bosom to be mingled with and purified by the living waters of the Gospel of Christ. Profoundly as I venerate the great truths and principles for which Protestantism stands, I am somewhat chilled by its inhumanity, its naked severity, its relentless rationality. If it feeds one half, perhaps the better half, of the soul, it starves the other. The religion of all men must be the religion of the whole man—Catholic in depth as well as in extension.

Could I dare admit that the Vatican Council had succeeded completely and finally in cutting Rome off from the ancient Catholic tradition; in inverting her constitution; in impeding the full influence of her past experience upon her future development, in damning the onward flow of all but the worst and most sterilising elements of that experience; in thus putting an end to her growth and expansion, then, indeed, by default, I should have to look away from this stunted trunk to the next heir of the Catholic tradition—to some of the lesser, but still living

167

and growing branches of Christendom. If I hold on, it is because I abhor runaway solutions, and spurious simplifications, whether ultramontane or schismatic, that would force a premature synthesis by leaving out all the intractable difficulties of the problem; that prefer a cheap logicality to the clash and confusion through which the immanent reason of the world works order out of the warring elements of a rich and fruitful chaos. The new must be made out of the old, must retain and transcend all its values.

As long as I think thus, it seems to me I must hold to the Roman Church. And if I will to do so, "Who shall separate us?" not twenty Popes nor a hundred excommunications. I belong to her in the only way that I care to belong to her—in spirit and in truth; by the bond of my free conviction that no bishop can snap. *Multi intus sunt qui foris videntur* —many who, with "the apostate Döllinger," seem to be outside are really inside. Many who, with their traducers, seem to be inside are really outside; for, what they hold to under the name of Catholicism is only a monopolised individualism—not the supremacy, but the absolute servitude and subjection of the *orbis terrarum*.

And so, Your Eminence, till better advised I will cling to my belief in the resurrection of the dead, and will dream my foolish dream of a day—not perhaps very far removed from the Greek Kalends—when the Catholic people represented by their bishops and their Pope will assemble, not to decide and impose points of theology, ethics and politics "under pain of eternal damnation," but to proclaim the gospel of God's Kingdom upon earth as it was proclaimed by Jesus Christ; to preach "unity in essentials, liberty in non-essentials, charity in all things."

Your Eminence, I call this a reply, yet strictly it is not so. Your Lenten Pastoral was not addressed to me, nor did I know of its existence till Lent was over and chance put it into my hands. I have thought it, however, more respectful and straightforward to write to you, rather than about

168

you or at you, and to ensure that my words shall reach you before they reach any one else, so that you may have ample time to keep them from the readers of your Pastoral should you think fit.

I am not so sanguine as to imagine that they will make the slightest impression on you, though from certain lines in your Pastoral I would fain believe that you were not all Cardinal, but had still some vulnerable heel of humanity in which a more skilful marksman than myself might lodge a shaft. Indeed, it is no impeachment of your sincerity to suspect that, in the depths of your subconsciousness, you agree with me more than you dare admit to yourself. For I know from personal experience how deep and sincere may be the conviction which, regarding the official view as identical with God's view, makes it a matter of conscience to shut one's eyes and ears to every suggestion of the possibility of any other view. I conceive it a false conscience, but as conscience in any form I respect it.

> Your Eminence's
> Fellow-servant in Christ,
> G. TYRRELL.

London, May 17, 1908

NOTE TO PAGE 73, LINE 27

Commenting on this passage, the American *Ecclesiastical Review* (September 1, 1908, p. 280), says: "This is hateful, for Fr. Tyrrell must know that such blasphemous interpretation as he here insinuates to be the practice of Rome, is one which would receive from the Pontiff and the Sacred Congregation, which represents the disciplinary tribunal of the Church, a condemnation not less severe than that which follows upon all other false teachers of religion."

Since the reviewer appeals to Caesar, to Caesar he shall go. I have before me a little tract called: *De la Dévotion au Pape.* It is by Arsène-Pierre Milet, Curé Doyen de La Roë, Diocese of Laval, with the *imprimatur* of the Archbishop of Tours. It is dedicated to Pius X, and published by Paul Salmon, of Tours, 1904. It consists in the development of the text Mark 12:30 applied to the Pope: "thou shalt love [him] with all thy mind, with all thy will, with all thy heart, and with all thy strength." These words refer directly to God; but "puisque le Pape représente Dieu sur la terre . . . nous devons l'aimer, quoique dans un degré subordonné, comme Dieu lui-meme—notre Père qui est au Ciel—de tout notre esprit, de toute notre volonté, de tout notre coeur, de toutes nos forces [since the Pope represents God on earth . . . we should love him, though to a lesser degree, as God himself—our Father who is in Heaven—with all our mind, with all our will, with all our heart, with all our strength]." For "except the mystery of the Real Presence, nothing makes us feel so well or touch so closely the presence of God as does the sight or even the thought of the Vicar of Christ." He is "the Father of all humanity; the Father of the simple faithful, as also of the priests and Bishops themselves":—

"Although there is not an absolute parity, yet in a certain sense one may say that as the Tabernacle is the home of Jesus the Victim, so the Palace of the Vatican at Rome is the home of Jesus the Teacher; that it is from this Palace, or rather Sanctuary, that since His Ascension our Lord Jesus Christ, the Divine Word, speaks to the world by the mouth of His Vicar, whether he be called Peter, or Pius IX, or Leo XIII, or Pius X." "What can be

170

more beautiful or touching than this parallelism? When we prostrate ourselves at the Tabernacle before the sacred hosts therein contained we adore our Lord in His Eucharistic Presence which is substantial and personal—when we fall at the Pope's feet to offer him the homage of our mind, and to accept his teachings, it is again, in a certain way, Jesus Christ Whom we adore in his Doctrinal Presence. In both cases we adore and confess the same Jesus Christ. Whence it follows by rigorous consequence that it is as impossible to be a good Christian without devotion to the Pope as without devotion to the Eucharist." "If, therefore, we truly love the Pope nothing will be dearer to us than the Pope's will; and even when obedience to the Pope means sacrifices we shall never hesitate to follow any direction whatsoever emanating from Rome. Every objection will be silenced, every reasoning will go for nothing [s'évanouira], every hesitation will yield before this unanswerable argument: 'God wills and commands it because the Pope wills and commands it.' Let us enter into the joys of the Pope; let us rejoice in his success and glory in his triumphs, but let us also share his anguish. . . . By the mere fact that he is the Vicar of Christ and His principal co-operant, he is an elect Victim and is *ex officio* nailed to the Cross. . . . Pope and Victim are two inseparable qualities."

As instances of those who have loved the Pope "with all their strength," we are invited "to hail with sentiments of respect, nay, "more, of the most profound veneration," the heroes of Castelficlardo, "Mentana," etc. "Ah, ils l'aimaient de toutes leurs forces puisqu'ils l'ont aimé jusqu'à l'effusion de leur sang [Yes, they loved him with all their strength since they loved him to the point of shedding their blood]." Those who cannot fight for the temporal power can pray and give money: "Prayer for the Pope is much, and would be enough were the Church a purely 'spiritual society'; but the Pope needs money to meet the great expenses of ecclesiastical administration." The pamphlet ends with a quotation from Mgr. Gay:—

"All the devotion to Jesus as Priest, Shepherd, and Father that enlightened faith can inspire is summed up practically and effectively in devotion to the Pope. . . . If one is devout to the Angels, the Pope is the visible Angel of the whole Church. If we are devout to the Saints, the Pope is on earth the source of sanctity, and is called 'his Holiness.' If one should have a devotion to the sacred Scriptures, the Pope is the living and speaking Bible. If it is a duty to be devout to the Sacraments, is not the Pope the Sacrament of Jesus by the mere fact that he is

His Vicar? "

It is not only the Archhishop of Tours who has blessed this blasphemous little tract. Cardinal Merry del Val writes to the author expressing the Pope's satisfaction with it as dictated by that spirit of intelligent piety which indicates a true Catholic and an exemplary priest.

"REVND° SIGNORE
SIGNORE ARSENIO PIETRO MILET
PARROCO DECANO DI LA ROÉ
(Laval—France)

"REVND° SIGNORE,—Compio con piacere l'incarico che il *Santo Padre* mi affida, di ringraziare, cioè, la S. V. per l'ommaggio che *Ella Gli* ha fatto del suo libro intitolato *De la dévotion au Pape*.— Grande fede certamente ed ardentissimo amore la *S. V.* ha dimostrato verso il Vicario di Cristo, per ossequio del quale ha dettate pagine tutte improntate allo spirito di quell' intelligente affetto che si addice al vero Cattolico ed all' esemplare sacerdote.—Laonde *Sua Santità* benedice di cuore a Lei ed all'egregio suo opuscolo,—ed io, nel renderla di ciò intesa, posso intanto a ripetermi con sensi di particulare stima.
Di V. S. Revnd°,
Affmo per servirla.
R. CARD. MERRY DEL VAL.
Roma, 23 Dicembre, I904."

[Reverend Sir, It is a pleasure to carry out the duty His Holiness has entrusted to me, to thank you ... for the homage you have rendered to His Holiness with your little book.... You have certainly shown great faith and most ardent love towards the Vicar of Christ ... in dictating pages so impregnated with that intelligent piety which indicates a true Catholic and an exemplary priest....]

The same key is struck by the *Corrispondenza Romana*, that faithful echo of the Pope's inmost heart, in the number for November 2I, 1908 :—"Il n'est pas inutile de vous résumer les sentiments et les ideés que j'ai entendu plusieurs fois exprimer ces jours-ci sur le Pape, sur le sens qu'un catholique français attache à ces expressions: aimer Pie X, suivre Pie X, fêter le jubilé de Pie X.

" Ce serait vraiment superficiel de faire tenir l amour de Pie X dans l'adresse d'hommages même enthousiastes, dans l'offrande de dons magnifiques, ou dans un pieux pèlerinage

auprès de son auguste personne. Certes, toutes ces manifestations affectueuses sont excellentes, mais combien passégères et
insuffisantes s'il ne s'y ajoutait la parfaite soumission de l'esprit
et une correspondance absolue des intentions et des volontés.

"Jubiler Pie X, c'est donc avant tout (ai-je entendu) se
surnaturaliser, car quel Pape fut plus surnaturel que celui-la?

... "Jubiler Pie X, si on ne le jubile pas que des lèvres, c'est
s'engager résolument dans ce chemin, avec les dispositions qui
conviennent d'obéissance confiante et de travail joyeux. Si on
me permet d'employer l'expression, imparfaite mais courante,
de 'la politique de Pie X,' jubiler Pie X c'est se faire les hommes
de cette politique, pour la faire mieux et plus vite réussir." [It is
not without use to sum up for you the sentiments and ideas that
I have frequently heard expressed in these days on the Pope,
following the meaning that a French Catholic attaches to these
expressions: loving Pius X, following Pius X, celebrating the
jubilee of Pius X. It would be truly superficial to restrict love for
Pius X to addressing even enthusiastic homages to him, to
offering him magnificent gifts, or to making a pious pilgrimage
to his august person. Of course, all these affectionate manifestations are excellent, but how fleeting and insufficient without
the addition of that perfect submission of will and an absolute
harmonization of intentions and desires.

To celebrate Pius X, is then (so I have heard) to supernaturalize
oneself, since which Pope was more supernatural than this one?

... To celebrate Pius X, if one does so with more than one's
lips, is to embark resolutely on that road, with the proper
dispositions of confident obedience and joyous labour. If I may
be allowed the expression, imperfect but current, "the policy of
Pius X," celebrating Pius X means becoming men of this policy,
to make it succeed better and quicker.]